Understanding How Issues in Business Ethics Develop

Understanding How Issues in Business Ethics Develop

Edited by

Ian W. Jones and Michael G. Pollitt

First published 2002 by
PALGRAVE MACMILLAN
Houndmills, Basingstoke, Hampshire RG21 6XS and
175 Fifth Avenue, New York, N.Y. 10010
Companies and representatives throughout the world

PALGRAVE MACMILLAN is the global academic imprint of the Palgrave Macmillan division of St. Martin's Press, LLC and of Palgrave Macmillan Ltd. Macmillan® is a registered trademark in the United States, United Kingdom and other countries. Palgrave is a registered trademark in the European Union and other countries.

ISBN 0–333–99810–3 hardback

This book is printed on paper suitable for recycling and made from fully managed and sustained forest sources.

A catalogue record for this book is available from the British Library.

Library of Congress Cataloging-in-Publication Data
Understanding how issues in business ethics develop / edited by
Michael Pollitt, Ian Jones.
      p.   cm.
'Based on the proceedings of a workshop on "Understanding how issues in business ethics develop" held on 7th December 2001 at New Hall, Cambridge'—Pref.
Includes bibliographical references and index.
ISBN 0–333–99810–3
1. Business ethics—Congresses.   2. Industrial management—Moral and ethical aspects—Congresses.   I. Pollitt, Michael G.   II. Jones, Ian, 1943–

HF5387 .U53 2002
174'.4—dc21

                                                                    2002074901

10   9   8   7   6   5   4   3   2   1
11   10   09   08   07   06   05   04   03   02

Printed and bound in Great Britain by
Antony Rowe Ltd, Chippenham and Eastbourne

Contents

List of Tables

List of Figures

Preface and Acknowledgements

This volume is based on the proceedings of a workshop on 'Understanding how issues in business ethics develop' held on 7 December 2001 at New Hall, Cambridge. The workshop was organised under the auspices of the ESRC Centre for Business Research (CBR) based in the Judge Institute of Management, Cambridge.

This workshop arose from the editors ongoing ESRC-funded research project on 'Ethics, Regulation and Globalisation', which seeks to further the understanding of how business ethics and related regulations are developing in an era of globalisation. This work seeks to combine biblical ethics, management practice and economics. The workshop is the third that we have organised since 1996. The first resulted in the publication of *The Role of Business Ethics and Economic Performance* (Macmillan, 1998) and the second in a special issue of *Long Range Planning* (vol. 32, no. 2, 1999) on 'Putting Values into Action'. This current volume brings together representatives from business, academia, NGOs and government with backgrounds in political science, law, economics, management and biological sciences.

The editors would like to acknowledge the support of the CBR for supporting their research programme since 1995 and for organising the day of the workshop. They especially thank the Director, Professor Alan Hughes, and the administrative secretary, Sue Moore, for her usual efficient organisation of the workshop. The editors wish to thank their families – Sara, Yvonne and Katherine and Nicholas – for their support during the process of readying the final draft. Above all, however, they acknowledge the effort of the contributors to the volume and their sustained support for the project.

Ian W. Jones
Michael G. Pollitt

List of Contributors

Peter Butler, Corporate Focus Director, Hermes Pensions Management Ltd and Chief Executive, Hermes Lens Asset Management Ltd.

Dr Andrew Clayton, Senior Policy Officer, Christian Aid.

Professor Simon Deakin, Assistant Director, Centre for Business Research and Robert Monks Professor of Corporate Governance, University of Cambridge.

Professor Michael Goldsmith, Professor of Law, Brigham Young University, US.

Professor Ian W. Jones, Visiting Professor of International Management, University of Exeter and Research Associate, Centre for Business Research, University of Cambridge.

Guy Jubb, Head of Corporate Finance, Standard Life Investments, UK.

Amy Bice Larson, Research Assistant, Faculty of Law, Brigham Young University, US.

Dr Sue Mayer, Executive Director of Genewatch UK and Senior Research Fellow, University of Sussex.

Sir Mark Moody-Stuart, Former Chairman, Royal Dutch Shell.

Dr Michael G. Pollitt, University Senior Lecturer in Business Economics, University of Cambridge and Research Associate, Centre for Business Research, University of Cambridge.

Graham Rodmell, UK Co-ordinator of Transparency International (UK) and Legal and Development Consultant.

R. Stephen Rubin, Chairman, Pentland Group plc.

Peter Siddall, Chair, Horticultural International.

Professor Bernard Taylor, Executive Director of the Centre for Board Effectiveness at Henley Management College, Henley-on-Thames.

Rodney Whittaker, Senior Vice President, Legal Operations International, GlaxoSmithKline plc.

Professor Robert M. Worcester, Chairman of MORI and Visiting Professor of Government at the London School of Economics.

1
Understanding How Issues in Business Ethics Develop: Introduction

Ian W. Jones and Michael G. Pollitt

Background

Corporate governance, executive pay, the use of child labour and control of industrial pollution are all examples of business ethics issues that today's companies must face. Such issues surface increasingly commonly in the running of companies, and managers and directors find them impossible to ignore. Indeed, there are many examples of companies becoming negatively associated with such issues: Robert Maxwell's Maxwell Communications Corporation (corporate governance),[1] British Gas (executive pay),[2] Nike (child labour)[3] and Union Carbide (industrial pollution).[4] However, while the issues themselves invite huge amounts of comment about how to deal with them, the process by which the issue develops over time is a much less discussed area. A key to being a sustainable company is the development of a capacity to understand and predict how such issues develop over time.

This volume examines the development of a number of the highest profile ethical issues facing companies over the past ten years in an attempt to draw lessons. In each case, we lay out the issue, discuss how it has developed, who has influenced the process and what the outcome for corporate behaviour has been. Each of the chapters discussing the issue is followed by a short comment from a discussant reflecting an alternative perspective on the development of the issue. Our focus is on issues which have primarily impacted on private companies but there are obviously lessons not only for the affected companies, but also for interested NGOs, government departments, regulatory agencies, the media and other parties interested in the development of business ethics issues.

Business ethics may be defined as 'the rules of conduct by which business decisions are made'.[5] Rules of conduct in business ethics often relate to a particular issue, such as the use of child labour. Business ethics are usually of greatest interest where the law is unclear in suggesting how companies should behave, or leaves it open to the interpretation of companies in the light of currently accepted practices among consumers, investors, employees and other non-governmental stakeholders such as NGOs. To take the issue of the use of child labour, this is much less of an issue in advanced countries than it used to be.[6] However, child labour is still an important issue for advanced-country companies with Third World supply chains because of the gap between acceptable practice in rich countries and the attitude of and enforcement of laws against such labour in developing countries such as India and Pakistan.

Issues in business ethics

This book has arisen from our ongoing work looking at the relationship between business ethics, economics and corporate strategy. We began by arguing that good business ethics can be justified within a shareholder value maximisation model as reflecting long-term enlightened self-interest (Jones and Pollitt, 1996). We suggested that economics could be used to justify business ethics at the individual, corporate and societal levels (reflected in both laws and social norms). We then went on to focus specifically on the economics and ethics of unfair competition within three types of business relationships: relationships within the supply chain, relationships with customers and relationships with rival companies (Jones and Pollitt, 1998a). In each case, we highlighted an example of a company that behaved in an ethical way within these relationships and one that did not. These comparisons strongly suggested that 'good' behaviour rather than 'bad' behaviour within business relationships could be made to pay.

We followed this with an edited volume in which a number of authors discussed the importance of business ethics in promoting improved economic performance (Jones and Pollitt, 1998b). Support for this view came from Adam Smith's book *The Theory of Moral Sentiments* (Eatwell, 1998) as well as modern economic theory (Casson, 1998) and empirical evidence on the importance of trust in business relationships (Deakin and Wilkinson, 1998). We also presented an examination of the demand and supply side forces driving the recent increase in interest in business ethics. On the demand side, we discussed the emergence of postmaterialism in advanced countries (Cohen, 1998) and increased shareholder activism (Sparkes, 1998), both of which were driven by a growing concern for the way economic activity is undertaken rather than just increasing consumption and wealth. On the supply side, we looked at the changing nature of the companies resulting in their increasing responsiveness to business ethics issues, particularly in a pluralist and multinational context (Wright, 1998; Hood, 1998).

Having suggested reasons why it is important for profit-maximising companies to pay attention to business ethics, we then moved on to look at how companies could put the values which lie behind good business ethics into practice. This involved a detailed case study on the implementation of an 'integrity' value at SmithKline Beecham (Jones and Pollitt, 1999a). This case study discussed how a new integrity value had been incorporated into the overall values of the company, how it had become part of the corporate change policy and how training and decision making had been influenced by the development of the value. The case study revealed how good business ethics could be operationalised within the company and how difficult it was to ensure that good business ethics entered into the lifeblood of the company. This paper became part of a set of papers that looked at how a range of organisations, including the pharmaceutical company Merck (Cuilla, 1999), a law practice (Harpur, 1999), and a hospital trust (Vallance, 1999), had connected their core values with their behaviour.

Examination of the experience of putting values into action led us to ask the question 'What drives particular issues in business ethics forward?' (Jones and Pollitt, 1999b). This question arises from the observation that business ethics are a part of corporate strategy and, as such, are subject to change and need continuous updating. The longest-lived companies are those that have developed a capacity to respond to new opportunities and threats as they arise. They are those that have the ability to deal with issues of what is acceptable behaviour and have come up with answers that are well received by their relevant stakeholder groups (shareholders, employees, government, local communities and so on). We developed a model of how business ethics develop that suggested that there was an ethical issue life cycle (*see* Figure 1.1).

Issues existed across a spectrum of seriousness of required company response that ran from voluntary best-practice response through to voluntary group response and on to mandatory response. Voluntary best-practice response involved visionary companies unilaterally taking action on particular issues; where trade associations took coordinated but voluntary action this was a voluntary group response. A mandatory response involved legal enforcement of corporate actions to deal with the issue.

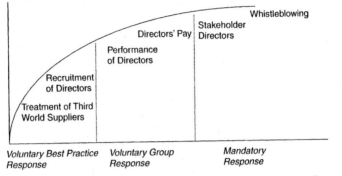

Y = Degree of Public Pressure

Whistleblowing

Stakeholder
Directors

Directors' Pay

Performance
of Directors

Recruitment
of Directors

Treatment of Third
World Suppliers

Voluntary Best Practice
Response

Voluntary Group
Response

Mandatory
Response

X = Seriousness of Industry Response

Figure 1.1   The ethical issue life cycle.

Source: Jones, I.W. and Pollitt, M.G. (1999b).

We went on to argue that there was a well-established pattern by which ethical issues started off on the left of the spectrum and moved towards the right. Indeed, one of the issues (directors' pay) that we suggested was then (1999) at the stage of voluntary group response has since moved towards a mandatory response within the UK. The suggestion that there were patterns in the development of business ethics led us to explore the specifics of the development of individual ethical issues as represented within this book.

Let us now turn to the specific questions that we seek to address in this volume.

Questions about the development of ethical issues

We seek to address five key questions about the development of issues in business ethics.

1. Why do certain ethical issues develop and not others?
2. Who is involved in the development of ethical issues?
3. When do the key stages in the development of an ethical issue occur?
4. How may the development of the issue be influenced?
5. What is the effect of the process on the final outcome of a debate?

Why do certain ethical issues develop and not others?

This book covers a wide range of ethical issues: the control of the power of executive directors, executive pay, the duties of directors, the efficacy of genetically modified (GM) crops, shareholder activism, the use of child labour, the control of industrial pollution and corporate bribery. Each of these issues is chosen because it has become a major issue leading to widespread debate within and outside the corporate sector, media interest, political involvement and, in most cases, significant changes in corporate behaviour.

However, why did these issues arise when they did? For instance, what triggered the huge interest in corporate governance in the UK since 1990, which events led up to the 1991 US Federal Sentencing Guidelines covering corporate misdemeanours, what has lain behind the various initiatives taken by the international sporting goods industry on child labour since the 1970s? And yet other issues, such as tobacco advertising and defence sales by advanced-country companies to dubious Third World regimes, have not taken off in the same way, in spite of the best efforts of activists who have seen many of their ambitions realised on other issues.[7] In this volume, we examine the origin of different issues in order to draw out lessons for the future.

Who is involved in the development of ethical issues?

We identify a number of important actors within the debates on the different issues we examine and the influence they have had on the different stages of the process. Looking across the chapters, there are roughly five key groups of actors.

First, there is *the business community* itself. This group is diverse but shares the common characteristic that it benefits from the economic activity associated with business. Thus, it consists of the corporations, their financial stakeholders (for example, shareholders, employees, suppliers), business professionals (for example, accountants and lawyers) and non-financial stakeholders (for example, local communities).

The second group is *the authorities*, such as regulators and government. These include financial regulators such as the Stock Exchange and the central bank which set reporting rules for companies. Government exercises its influence through its ability to bring forward credible legislation and through its ability to form committees of investigation (Ayres and Braithwaite, 1992).

A third group consists of *public opinion formers*, such as the media, NGOs and 'popular feeling'. This group also includes Opposition politicians who can often effectively use the media to bring pressure on the government (for example, over executive pay in the UK in 1994–5).

A fourth group is *international organisations*, such as international NGOs (for instance, Greenpeace) and international institutions such as the United Nations (UN), World Bank and Organisation for Economic Co-operation and Development (OECD). This group has been particularly significant on issues involving the actions of multinationals in developing countries, such as the UN on the issue of child labour (Clayton, this volume) and the OECD on bribery of foreign-government officials overseeing multinational contracts (Rodmell, this volume).

The final group is *events*. These have the effect of drawing attention to particular issues and precipitating action in reaction to the raised perception of a problem. One can give examples of spectacular corporate failures (often triggered by economic recessions) leading to improved corporate governance and environmental disasters leading to interest to corporate actions. Examples are: the 1990 collapse of the Maxwell empire in the UK (Jones and Pollitt, this volume); the aftermath of the corporate involvement in the 1974 Watergate scandal in the US (Goldsmith, this volume); and the effect of Shell's attempt to dispose of the Brent Spar oil rig in the Atlantic in 1995 (Moody-Stuart, this volume).

When do the key stages in the development of an ethical issue occur?

This question raises two issues: what are the key stages in the development of an ethical issue and what determines their timing? In the next chapter, we identify a number of different stages in the development of the corporate governance reports in the UK. These are: an initial interest phase followed by the formation of a committee; the formulation of terms of reference for the enquiry; a period of deliberation; the process of drafting and taking comments on an initial draft; presentation of the findings; subsequent debate and implementation by the affected parties (in this case companies changing their board procedures and reporting).

While this particular sequence of events is specific to this class of issues, in the UK the basic process of issue identification, analysis and implementation of solutions is replicated in many issues where there has eventually been a resolution. It is reflected in the issue of GM crops, corporate bribery and use of child labour, discussed in later chapters. The exact trigger points for each of the stages of the debate lie in the details of the particular case. However, many issues do follow a time-table once the process of analysis has been identified – for example, the corporate governance debates in the UK had a timetable set by the sponsoring group behind the investigating committees. Timetables also emerge in government and corporate sponsored investigations into different issues – such as the timetable for the coming into force of the OECD Anti-bribery Convention following its ratification.

How may the development of the issue be influenced?

The identification of the key actors in the debates about corporate governance and an awareness of the different stages in the development of the debate permit a better understanding of how the process may be influenced. The aim of this volume is to bring readers to this position of understanding. There are many examples in this volume of highly effective influence by one or more parties within a debate.

Thus, we see the influence of accountants and lawyers in the corporate governance debates in the UK, NGOs leading successful campaigns on GM crops in the UK, government agencies prompting change on corporate responsibility in the US, companies effectively engaging on the issue of child labour in Pakistan and activist fund managers addressing underperformance of management in portfolio companies. These observations of what made for a successful influence are drawn out in the chapters and in the conclusion. The important point to note at the outset is that it is possible to identify a successful attempt to influence by almost every major actor when looking at the range of debates covered here.

This does not imply that any given actor could be influential on any given debate. For instance, it is difficult to see how GM-crop companies could have prevented a consumer backlash against purchasing GM foodstuffs. However, it does suggest that there are more or less effective ways to engage in the debate as it develops. What is clear is that an understanding of how the process of development of an issue works is crucial to maintaining an individual company's competitive advantage over its rivals.

What is the effect of the process on the final outcome of a debate?

We are not concerned here with what the right answer was in a particular debate. We are interested in identifying how the *process* of development affected the final outcome. Each of the debates considered yields insights into this. Processes that are heavily reliant on business input yield pro-business outcomes, as in the case of the Cadbury Report on corporate governance. Processes that are highly inclusive tend not to be as radical as those that are driven by radicals. Contrast between the radical outcome of the GM debate in the UK, which was successfully managed by NGOs (Mayer, this volume) and the company law review that involved wide consultation and the inclusion of NGOs *and* companies (Jones and Pollitt, this volume). Processes where the parties invite regulation tend to lead to regulatory solutions, illustrated by the lobbying by large corporations in the US over the Federal Sentencing Guidelines (Goldsmith, this volume). Each of the papers in the volume examines the process and the final outcome, and allows the reader to connect the two. We return to the overall lessons in the conclusion.

An overview of the chapters

In Chapter 2, we develop the idea of a process of influence in the course of development of debates in business ethics and provide a framework for analysing the development of such issues. We investigate the influences behind five major investigations into corporate governance in the UK since 1990: the Cadbury, Greenbury, Hampel and Turnbull committees and the Company Law Review. These investigations variously considered the control of executive power, the reporting of executive pay and the legal duties of directors. In each case, we examine the roles of business, the authorities, public opinion and events in shaping the course of the investigation, its conclusions and its impact. The picture that emerges is one where the origins of the formation of the investigating committee, its membership and its mode of operation strongly influence its recommendations and effectiveness. We draw conclusions that contrast the strong influence of the accountancy and legal professions in shaping the debate and the varied influence of the authorities, the media and events. A surprising finding is that the target of the investigations – corporations – exerted a rather weak influence on the process. In commenting on the chapter, Bob Worcester notes that public opinion is not interested in corporate governance *per se* but in the results of poor governance. The reputation of business depends not on corporate governance changes but on the avoidance of scandals.

In Chapters 3 and 4, we examine the role of public opinion and NGOs in shaping ethical debates. Sue Mayer (in Chapter 3) examines the role of NGOs in the debate about GM foods in the UK which reached a hiatus in 1998 and 1999. The agricultural biotechnology industry argues that such foods have consumer benefits and are essential to feeding the world. However, the proposed introduction of genetically modified (GM) foods has been met with such hostility in Europe that GM ingredients are no longer used by the major food producers in the UK. This was a result of a high profile NGO campaign. Mayer argues that this was successful because it resonated with many public concerns – the ability of science to predict harm; whether institutions will act impartially; whether markets will allow choice; how international trade rules affect consumers; and the exclusion of ethical matters from decisions. She suggests that the industry's failure to win the arguments so far has been because it did not engage with the underlying issues of who bears the risks and takes the benefits. The conclusion is that industry will have to engage more deeply in a debate about technology assessment if GM crops are to have a future in Europe. In response, Peter Siddall offers a robust defence of the industry position on the arguments for the introduction of GM crops in the UK, noting that while Europe has expressed its concerns, the world acreage under GM crops, particularly in China and the Americas, has continued to grow rapidly.

Andrew Clayton (in Chapter 4) discusses the development of the issue of the use of child labour in the Third World within export sectors. He discusses the involvement of many different organisations, including human-rights groups, development agencies, governments, trade unions, UN agencies and the private sector, in addressing the issue.

The result has been a greater public and business awareness of the issue and business engagement in a number of positive initiatives. What he makes evident is that the issue is much less clear cut than it might at first appear and that well-meaning attempts to eradicate it can have negative consequences for the children involved. Clayton reviews a number of ongoing initiatives that illustrate the positive role business can play in addressing the issue. These include the successful Sialkot programme for the phasing out of child labour in the football stitching industry in Pakistan which has involved the cooperation of international NGOs (led by Save the Children), the local government and the major branded sportsgoods' companies that purchase many of the footballs. Stephen Rubin (a member of the Sports Industry Association) follows this paper with an industry response discussing how his company (Pentland Industries) approached the issue of child labour. Fascinatingly, he discusses an initial attempt to reduce child labour within his supply chain, which backfired and had to be revised, as an illustration of how well-intentioned but inadequately researched policies can be counterproductive for the very groups they are intended to help.

Chapters 5 and 6 move the focus to ways in which government actions can effect the development of ethical issues. Michael Goldsmith and Amy Brice Larson (Chapter 5) discuss the impact of law enforcement on corporate ethics. The Watergate scandal revealed undisclosed illegal campaign contributions to domestic and foreign governments and politicians. This led to the *Foreign Corrupt Practices Act* of 1978 that prohibited bribery by US companies of foreign government officials. He traces how this set in train a sequence of reforms that eventually led to the US Department of Justice issuing its 1991 Federal Sentencing Guidelines. These guidelines combined a carrot and stick approach to organisational crime, the stick being large fines (up to $75m per illegal action) and the carrot being a culpability score which may mitigate the fine by up to 95 per cent. A key element in mitigation is the demonstration of an 'effective' corporate compliance (or integrity) programme – that the company actively encourages a high standard of internal ethical behaviour. The guidelines are careful to set some steps which 'effective' compliance programmes should be expected to demonstrate without specifying the exact nature of the programme. The effect of these guidelines has been to engineer the widespread introduction of compliance programmes within large US companies and to cause significantly improved ethical standards within companies. In response, Simon Deakin acknowledges the potential effectiveness of the law in driving changes in corporate ethics. He goes on to discuss the capacity for health and safety legislation to change corporate behaviour and how UK law may be further strengthened in this area.

Graham Rodmell (Chapter 6) discusses the debates behind the recent OECD anti-bribery convention. This convention essentially pledges all OECD countries to introduce legislation similar to the provisions of the US *Foreign Corrupt Practices Act* into their national legislation. He illustrates how multilateral government action is likely to bring about a sharp increase in the pressure on companies to set the same standards of ethical behaviour towards competition for contracts in developing countries as they do in host countries. This has been given new impetus in the UK by the inclusion of the provisions of the convention in the *Anti-terrorism, Crime and Security Act* 2001 in the UK.

Rodney Whittaker from GlaxoSmithKline gives a company perspective on how the enforcement of the provisions of the US *Foreign Corrupt Practices Act* and the incentives provided by the Federal Sentencing Guidelines have translated into training for line managers within his company. He makes clear that the law has a powerful impact on in-company training.

The next two chapters move the focus to the business community's response to pressure to raise its ethical standards. Peter Butler (Chapter 7), from the activist fund manager, Hermes Lens, unpacks the issue of how shareholder activism is a growing force behind the pressure on companies to be more ethical. As a manager of a portfolio of around £35bn ($70bn), he outlines the Hermes Lens approach to engagement with portfolio company managers. In particular, he illustrates how managers can be encouraged to consider the ethical risks they face and how they can be held to account for poor decisions. He is clear that pension fund holders are increasingly putting pressure on their fund managers to be more activist and that conventional passive investment is likely to become less popular. Hermes Lens has been able to out-perform significantly by virtue of its activism, leading by changing portfolio company behaviour in ways that impact positively on share prices. Guy Jubb, from the 'conventional' fund manager Standard Life, supports Butler's basic position, indicating how issues to do with business ethics are increasingly prominent in the thinking and actions of firms like his.

Sir Mark Moody-Stuart (Chapter 8) shares some of his experiences as the chairman of Shell during and following their *annus horribilis* of 1995. In that year, the company faced customer boycotts and high-profile negative media coverage due to their proposal to dispose of the Brent Spar oil platform in the Atlantic and their apparent support for the Nigerian Government against local people claiming compensation for environmental damage caused by their oil drilling. The company had previously had a good ethical and environmental reputation but found itself having to completely rethink its approach to engagement with interested stakeholders. The result was the introduction of a new process of wide consultation with NGOs and other interested parties. By 1998, during which year the financial performance of the company was deteriorating, some were saying that the company had lost direction. Sir Mark shares how he realised the need to take action that both improved the financial position and did not lead to the processes of stakeholder engagement being discredited. He ends by suggesting how such stakeholder engagement is essential for companies such as his, that aspire to be 'companies of choice' for consumers and employees. In his comments, Bernard Taylor is impressed by the recent changes at Shell and offers a checklist of action points for company managers looking to learn the lessons of Shell's experiences in 1995.

In sum, the chapters offer outsider and insider perspectives on the development of a number of important recent debates in business ethics. There is much in them about how companies responded effectively to the issues as they developed. In our conclusion, we draw out some of the common themes raised by the authors across the different debates with a view to helping companies and those who advise them develop the capacity to respond more effectively to ethical challenges as they arise.

Notes

1   *See* Jones and Pollitt (1996).
2   *See* Whysall (1998).
3   *See* N. Gibbs and J.F. Dickerson, 'Cause Celeb: Two high-profile endorsers are props in a worldwide debate over sweatshops and the use of child labor', *Time*, vol. 147, issue 25, 17 June, 1996, p. 28.
4   *See* Shrivastava (1995).
5   Jones and Pollitt (1998, p. 4).
6   *See* Shelburne (2001).
7   As Meyer (this volume) points out, NGOs run hundreds of campaigns each year within advanced countries, yet only a few gain national public attention.

References

Ayres, I. and Braithwaite, J. (1992) *Responsive Regulation*, Oxford: Oxford University Press.

Casson, M. (1998) 'The Economics of Ethical Leadership', in Jones, I.W. and Pollitt, M.G. (eds) *The Role of Business Ethics in Economic Performance*, Basingstoke: Palgrave Macmillan.

Cohen, M. (1998) 'Evidence of a New Environmental Ethic: Assessing the Trend towards Investor and Consumer Activism', in Jones, I.W. and Pollitt, M.G. (eds) *The Role of Business Ethics in Economic Performance*, Basingstoke: Palgrave Macmillan.

Cuilla, J.B. (1999) 'The importance of leadership in shaping business values', *Long Range Planning*, vol. 32, no. 2, pp. 166–72.

Deakin, S. and Wilkinson, F. (1998) 'Cooperation, Contract Law and Economic Performance', in Jones, I.W. and Pollitt, M.G. (eds) *The Role of Business Ethics in Economic Performance*, Basingstoke: Palgrave Macmillan.

Eatwell, J. (1998) 'Ethics and Self-Interest', in Jones, I.W. and Pollitt, M.G. (eds) *The Role of Business Ethics in Economic Performance*, Basingstoke: Palgrave Macmillan.

Harpur, O.M. (1999) 'Decision making conditioned by values: case study evidence from the legal profession', *Long Range Planning*, vol. 32, no. 2, pp. 207–16.

Hood, N. (1998) 'Business Ethics and Transnational Companies', in Jones, I.W. and Pollitt, M.G. (eds) *The Role of Business Ethics in Economic Performance*, Basingstoke: Palgrave Macmillan.

Jones, I.W. and Pollitt, M.G. (1996), 'Economics, Ethics and Integrity in Business' *Journal of General Management*, vol. 21, no. 3, pp. 30–47.

Jones, I.W. and Pollitt, M.G. (1998a) 'Ethical and Unethical Competition: Establishing the Rules of Engagement', *Long Range Planning*, vol. 31, no. 5, pp. 703–10.

Jones, I.W. and Pollitt, M.G. (1998b) (eds), *The Role of Business Ethics in Economic Performance*, Basingstoke: Palgrave Macmillan/St Martin's Press.

Jones, I.W. and Pollitt, M.G. (1999a) 'From Promise to Compliance: The development of "Integrity" at SmithKline Beecham', *Long Range Planning*, vol. 32, no. 2, pp. 190–8.

Jones, I.W. and Pollitt, M.G. (1999b) *The Development of Ethical Issues facing Boards of Directors: A model with implications*, ESRC Centre for Business Research Working Paper No. 151.

Shelburne, R.C. (2001) 'An explanation of the international variation in the prevalence of child labour', *World Economy*, vol. 24, issue 3, pp. 359–78.

Shrivastava, P. (1995) 'Industrial/environmental crises and corporate social responsibility', *Journal of Socio-Economics*, vol. 24, issue 1, pp. 211–36.

Smith, A. (1759) *The Theory of Moral Sentiments*, ed. D.D. Raphael and A.L. Macfie, Oxford: Clarendon.

Sparkes, R. (1998) 'The Challenge of Ethical Investment: Activism, Assets and Analysis', in Jones, I.W. and Pollitt, M.G. (eds) *The Role of Business Ethics in Economic Performance*, Basingstoke: Palgrave Macmillan.

Vallance, E. (1999) 'Sleeping with the enemy or learning from each other? Sharing ethical experiences between the public and private sectors', *Long Range Planning*, vol. 32, no. 2, pp. 199–206.

Whysall, P. (1998) 'Ethical Relationships in Retailing: Some Cautionary Tales', *Business Ethics – A European Review*, vol. 7, no. 2, pp. 103–10.

Wright, C. (1998) 'Business Ethics and Corporate Culture', in Jones, I.W. and Pollitt, M.G. (eds) *The Role of Business Ethics in Economic Performance*, Basingstoke: Palgrave Macmillan.

2

Who Influences Debates in Business Ethics? An Investigation into the Development of Corporate Governance in the UK since 1990

Ian W. Jones and Michael G. Pollitt

Corporate governance debates in the UK

Corporate governance has been defined as 'the system by which companies are directed and controlled'.[1] As such, corporate governance relates to the organisation and functioning of the company board of directors. In the UK, the debate about corporate governance has a number of key elements.[2]

1. The *duties of a director* with respect to the various stakeholders in a company.
2. The composition of the board with respect to the number of *non-executive* (or outside) *directors* in comparison with executive directors who are also full-time managers with the company. These non-executive directors may be *independent* in the sense that they have no previous or other ongoing connection with the company.
3. The presence and composition of various subcommittees of the main company board: namely the audit, nomination and remuneration committees. The *audit committee* is responsible for reviewing the internal and external audits of the company. The *nomination committee* recommends new directors for appointment to the board. The *remuneration committee* recommends the compensation packages to be offered to the executive directors.
4. The *separation of the roles* of chairman of the board from that of chief executive.

5. The consideration of the *appropriate degree of internal control* within a company.
6. The *degree of reporting* on matters of board composition and policy in the annual report.

The 1990s have witnessed a major upheaval in the way corporations are governed in the UK. Beginning with the Cadbury Report in 1992, many corporations have been faced with a series of major changes in their board structure and their degree of reporting on issues of audit, remuneration and the process of the appointment of directors. The Cadbury Report was a response to the widespread view that UK corporate governance lagged behind that in other countries and that this lack of best practice had contributed to some of the spectacular collapses of listed corporations – such as Asil Nadir's Polly Peck, BCCI, Coloroll and Maxwell Communications Corporation.[3] That report was followed by three more major reports: Greenbury (1995), Hampel (1998) and Turnbull (1999). The Greenbury Report responded to concern about the level of executive pay rises, especially in the privatised utilities. The Hampel Report reviewed the progress of companies in responding to the Cadbury and Greenbury Reports and made some suggestions for improvement. The Turnbull Report addressed the important issue of how to implement best-practice systems of internal control. Currently (2002), the Labour Government is completing a wide ranging review of company law that addresses aspects of corporate governance within the wider context of the *Companies Act*.[4]

The result of all this activity is that UK corporate governance ranks as the most open and transparent system of any in the leading industrialised countries. The UK is now ranked ahead of the US in terms of the quality of the environment facing investors, on the basis of the governance practices of the firms they were most likely to invest in.[5]

The issue at the heart of the development of corporate governance in the UK has been the encouragement of the appropriate exercise of power by executive directors. While much of the focus has been directed at the limitation of the risk of potential abuses of executive power, the various governance reports have sought to encourage executives to see best-practice governance as an aid to good performance.[6] The issue of the appropriate exercise of executive power is a key issue in business ethics or the 'rules of conduct according to which business decisions are made'.[7]

In what follows, we wish to identify the major influences on the development of the issue of corporate governance in the UK. Our aim is to attempt to identify who and what have shaped the debate about this important aspect of business ethics in the UK. We seek to do this in the context of an interest in establishing how companies might strategically interact with emerging ethical issues.

We will focus on the conduct of the committees charged with drafting the governance reports. We base our comments on interviews with members of each of the corporate governance committees and an analysis of the how the issue played out in the newspapers over the period. The aim is to help those charged with responding to ethical issues in order that they may best deal with them in the future. In the next section, we lay out our organising framework. The subsequent four sections discuss the Cadbury, Greenbury, Hampel and Turnbull reports in turn. We then apply our framework to the Company Law Review. The last section concludes by drawing together our main findings.

A framework for analysis

Our concern is to track the influences surrounding what have turned out to be the central focuses for debating the ethical issues surrounding the behaviour of UK companies since 1990. We do not seek to discuss the ethical issues themselves but to look at what has influenced how they were discussed in the UK and how these influences have shaped how the issues have been dealt with. Our desire is to begin to identify where ethical issues facing companies come from, how they develop over time and what determines how they will necessitate change for the company. We do this by identifying the key sources of influence in the corporate governance debate and by breaking down the phases of each governance committee's work into a number of stages. In our subsequent detailed discussions of each of the Committee's work, this provides us with a framework for presenting our findings on what were the most significant influences on the development of the process at the key stages.

The conduct of our investigation

Much has been written on the content of the different governance reports in the UK but very little has been written on how the issues have developed.[8] We initially collected empirical evidence through publicly available information, amplified by lightly structured interviews with key individuals in the field, taken from ethical and corporate pressure groups and a business school. This preliminary investigation led to the development of a semi-structured questionnaire for conducting personal interviews with members of the committees and undertaken jointly by the authors. Following a 'grounded' approach, the questionnaires were an *aide-memoire* to ensure that relevant matters were investigated. Consistent with this approach, a model was developed for the principal factors in volved. Our approach was then to interview a member of each committee, other than the chair. The rationale of approaching someone other than the chair was that that person would give a view of how the committee was conducted and whether the prevailing view (which might be assumed to be consistent with the view of the chair) was held throughout the committee. The selection of who to interview was on the basis of selecting accessible individuals known to be thoughtful opinion leaders in the area.

The influence groups

In the course of our investigation, we have come across a number of significant influence groups in the area of corporate governance. We identify and discuss each of these in turn below. The influences can be roughly grouped into four sets: business (including corporates, non-financial stakeholders, financial stakeholders and professionals), authorities (government and regulators), public opinion (media, NGOs and popular feeling) and exogenous factors (events).

Corporates

By this we mean the companies affected by corporate governance debates directly (as opposed to other companies such as pension funds concerned about the governance of companies they invest in) and key executives within them, such as executive directors. This group also includes organisations that represent company interests in the UK, such as the Confederation of British Industry (CBI)[9] and the Institute of Directors (IOD).[10] Of particular concern are the publicly quoted companies most affected by the Governance debates, though all commercial organisations, small and medium enterprises, and mutually owned societies can be considered part of this group.

Non-financial stakeholders

These are those who have an interest or concern in the business different from ownership. This group includes a wide group of people whose economic welfare depends on, or is affected by the action of companies. This group includes supplier companies, employees (and their unions), customers and those responsible for the environment.

Financial stakeholders

This group includes pension funds and investment trusts. It is concerned with the impact of poor governance on the performance of the shares held within the portfolios they own or manage on behalf of others. They may also be influenced, more indirectly, by consumer pressure from individual investors who want to invest in responsible companies. This group includes 'activist' fund managers such as Hermes, who have publicly opposed boards with poor performance records. This group is represented by the Association of British Insurers (ABI)[11] and the National Association of Pension Funds (NAPF).[12]

Professionals

Professionals are engaged in a vocation especially requiring advanced training or knowledge. In the case of corporate governance, these are, particularly, the accountancy and law professions. As individuals, professionals may work for business services firms or directly as executives for corporates. These groups have influenced the governance debate via their professional bodies, namely the Institute of Chartered Accountants for England and Wales (ICAEW)[13] and the Law Society.[14] The ICAEW claims to have at least one member on the board of all the leading companies in the UK.

Politicians

Politicians have influenced the corporate governance debate both in Government and in Opposition. In Opposition, politicians may cooperate with the media to raise business issues which might embarrass the Government (such as with the issue of executive pay discussed below). In Government, politicians have the additional support of the Civil Service in organising assessments of the scope for change in the law and in threatening to enact legislation if the corporate sector does not take action. Government ministers can put high-level pressure on the business community to act (such as the then Deputy Prime Minister was able to put on the CBI over executive pay in the run up to the Greenbury Committee). Other types of ministerial involvement may come through the explicit linking of business issues with a wider political agenda (as the first Labour Industry Secretary, Margaret Beckett, did in linking corporate governance issues to the stakeholding philosophy at the heart of the early Blair government).

Regulators

Corporates are regulated both by statute and by voluntary agreement. In the area of corporate governance, we identify key City regulators as being significant influences. The Bank of England (and later the Financial Services Authority)[15] was concerned about the role of poor corporate governance in corporate bankruptcy and fraud in its role as supervisor of the financial integrity of the City of London. The Bank of England had a traditional role as the overall City regulator and had set up Pro-NED, an organisation promoting the use of independent non-executive directors. The Stock Exchange[16] was similarly concerned and has significant influence on company behaviour via its control of the listing rules, such as on reporting in company accounts, with which companies must comply if their shares are to be traded on the London Stock Exchange. The Financial Reporting Council (FRC)[17] has also been a significant player in the corporate governance debates. The FRC incorporates the Accounting Standards Board (ASB) and the Financial Reporting Review Panel. It is an independent overseer of financial reporting in the UK and is sponsored jointly by the accountancy profession, the City and the Government. It was established in 1990 in the wake of high-profile business failures and reflects shared accountancy profession and Stock Exchange interests in financial reporting.

Media

The media includes the main means of mass communication. In the area of corporate governance, this has particularly included the financial press and the popular newspapers who highlighted the issue of executive pay as it related to particular highly paid individuals. The media has a role in picking up ideas which are of public interest and in giving 'airtime' to individuals with points of view which challenge the Establishment.

Non-governmental organisations (NGOs)

NGOs are 'private organisations that pursue activities to relieve suffering, promote the interests of the poor, protect the environment, provide basic social services, or undertake community development'.[18] Within corporate governance, NGOs would include lobby groups (not included above) and research groups concerned with governance, corporate social responsibility or ethics. These are usually non-commercial, but in common with many charities may include a commercial activity. A particularly notable NGO involved with corporate governance is the Pensions and Investment Research Centre (PIRC),[19] which has campaigned on various issues to do with poor corporate governance.

Popular feeling

This is the prevalent view or views held by the majority of the community with respect to corporate governance or which relate more widely to corporate conduct or even political issues that touch on corporate governance. It acts as a spur to media reporting and NGO activity and also political concern. However, it may in turn be influenced by the highlighting of issues by other groups.

Exogenous factors

These are occurrences believed to be outside the control of any of the individual actors within the economic system. Events such as a spectacular collapse of a high-profile company may trigger a political or media reaction. They may also include the general state of the macro-economy and the stock market.[20] This may affect the economy directly through its effect on issues of public concern or indirectly through its impact on corporate performance and company failure rates. We would usually expect failures to be lower in economic booms and, hence, concern for corporate governance to be correspondingly low. We would also expect public acceptance of 'normal' business practices to be higher when the economy and the stock market are doing well and society more generally is seen to be benefiting from business activity.

The enquiry process

Based on our observations of the actual enquiry processes, we now set out the key stages of the process by which each of the governance committees operated. We discuss each stage in chronological order.

Initial interest

This refers to the stage before the committee is set up, during which those influence groups who feel strongly that they want something done about a particular issue make their views known. The fact that this initial interest is significant is what brings the committee into being.

Formation of the committee

This stage includes the appointment of the chair, key members and all the members of the committee. The experience and view of corporate governance represented in the composition of the committee is a significant factor in setting the nature of the discussion and in shaping the final report. The choice of who to chair the committee, given their pivotal role in inviting others on to the committee and in discerning consensus among mostly lay members, is very important.

Terms of reference

Here we mean the remit given to the committee. This is the official terms of reference given to the committee but also includes any redefinition or elaboration that the committee may set itself, at the outset, as its working terms of reference.

Deliberation

This relates to the hows and wherefores of the principal workings of the committee, including the nature of informal and formal consultation and the issuing of draft reports. This period covers the longest part of the life span of the committee.

Compilation of the final report

This is how the final report is put together and what influences are reflected most strongly in the written conclusions, given the process of consultation that has occurred following the issuing of the draft reports.

The content of the final report

This stage represents what the final report contains. The influences on it are discussed under the previous heading. In the following sections, we note what the main conclusions of the committee reports were.

Presentation of the final report

This relates to how the committee's final report is launched into the public domain. This includes who is present at the launch, who presents it and the willingness to involve the media at this final stage. This would include any ongoing promotion of the report by the chair of the committee and his willingness to engage in subsequent debate surrounding the report.

Debate

This stage refers to the debate following the launch of the report. This identifies who the most influential shapers of the debate were. This phase may last several months.

Implementation

This is the final phase and refers to who takes the responsibility for seeing through the enactment of the report's principle recommendations. This phase can be a significant part of the process, with the committees even staying in operation for a period after the publication of the report. The normal expectation, however, would be that the report is received by the sponsoring institutions and responsibility for overseeing the implementation process passes to them.

In our analysis we will conclude our discussion of each governance report with an assessment of the extent to which each of the influence groups has influenced each stage of the enquiry process. We will assign one of four levels of influence to each group at each stage based on our assessment of the evidence.

The beginning of a quiet revolution – The Cadbury Committee

The UK economy experienced a prolonged period of economic growth from 1981 to 1989 under the Conservative Administration of Mrs Thatcher. However, towards the end of that period the economy began to show signs of overheating, especially in 1987 and 1988, with sharp rises in GDP growth and asset prices. High inflation and negative growth were experienced in 1990 and 1991.[21] Company failures rose and there were some spectacular collapses including Asil Nadir's Polly Peck, Coloroll, Robert Maxwell's MCC and the $8bn failure of the Bank of Credit and Commerce International (BCCI).[22] These collapses were all characterised by a number of similarities: a recent clean bill of health from auditors, a flamboyant and powerful leader, a lack of action from non-executive directors and little involvement with institutional investors.[23]

These collapses caused widespread public concern, not only because of the involvement of thousands of deposit holders in the collapse of BCCI and thousands of company pensioners in the collapse of the Maxwell Empire, but because of the perception that UK industry was doing badly economically, compared with other countries in continental Europe.[24]

The City was prompted to respond.[25] In May 1991, the Financial Reporting Council, the London Stock Exchange and the accountancy profession set up a committee on the Financial Aspects of Corporate Governance. The Financial Reporting Council was concerned about the absence of accurate reporting in the major cases of failure, which would have allowed investors to spot the warning signs. The Stock Exchange was concerned about the reputation of the City with investors. The accountancy profession was concerned about the potential liability faced by auditors who signed off a set of accounts which turned out be a misrepresentation of the facts, and about losing its self-regulatory role.[26] The chairman of the Financial Reporting Council, Sir Ron Dearing, approached Sir Adrian Cadbury to chair the committee. Cadbury had been Chairman of Cadbury Schweppes Plc and was then Chairman of Pro-NED, a Bank of England-sponsored organisation set up to promote the use of independent non-executive directors in the boardroom. Cadbury had authored a book on how to be an effective company chairman[27] and was a respected figure in the City, having been head of a family firm.

It was Cadbury himself who drew up the terms of reference for the committee, which were:

> To consider the following issues in relation to the financial reporting and accountability and to make recommendations on good practice:
>
> (a) the responsibilities of executive and non-executive directors for reviewing and reporting on performance to shareholders and other financially interested parties; and the frequency, clarity and form in which information should be provided;
>
> (b) the case for audit committees of the board, including their composition and role;
>
> (c) the principal responsibilities of auditors and the extent and value of audit;
>
> (d) the links between shareholders, boards, and auditors;
>
> (e) any other relevant matters.
>
> (Cadbury Report, 1992, Appendix, p. 61)

The committee was formed with members[28] drawn from the CBI, the accountancy profession, finance directors, academia, the Bank of England, the Stock Exchange, the Institute of Directors, institutional investors[29] and the Law Society. The Department of Trade and Industry (DTI)[30] provided a secretary to the committee, who acted as their observer.

The committee met monthly and produced an interim report in May 1992.[31] It was an instant literary success with 13 500 copies being distributed during the consultation period. In the interim report, the committee came out in favour of self-regulation and put a stress on the role of non-executive directors.[32] It did not recommend that shareholders have a right to vote on executive pay packages[33] or seek to reverse the Caparo Case, in which the House of Lords ruled that auditors have a duty of care only to management not to shareholders.[34] The enforcement mechanism for the new rules was to be that a statement of the extent of compliance with the Code in a Company's Annual Report was to be made a Stock Exchange listing requirement.[35]

Non-executive directors lay at the centre of the committee's interim proposals.[36] There were to be at least three independent non-executives on the board. The role of chief executive and chairman should be split with a non-executive becoming chairman. They were to form the membership of audit, remuneration and nomination committees. Audit committees would review the internal control systems in the company, remuneration committees would set pay for executive directors and nomination committees would propose candidates to fill board vacancies.

The interim report attracted various types of criticism – indeed only one in five reactions to the interim report registered strong support.[37] From the business community there was the charge that the system it advocated was too bureaucratic. The CBI and the Institute of Directors were both critical of this.[38] The CBI, in particular, fought for the removal of the requirement that compliance with the code should be part of the listing requirements for the Stock Exchange.[39] Cadbury himself and the CBI traded arguments in public about this.[40] Some investment groups suggested that it did not go far enough in recommending shorter service contracts for directors, improved disclosure of executive pay in corporate accounts and better financial information.[41] Indeed, there was some doubt as to whether the fundamental problem of internal control was being addressed.[42] Auditors felt that the requirement on them to verify compliance with the code was difficult to implement because of the difficulty of giving verifiable opinions on whether the company was a going concern or had appropriate internal controls.[43] Other commentators raised the issue of whether Cadbury's faith in self-regulation would mean that he would not go far enough (Finch, 1992). Indeed, the fact that Cadbury obviously looked to the US for ideas must have limited his radicalism.[44]

Cadbury continued to stress to those in the business community who thought the idea of a code was too bureaucratic that those who do not understand business so well, and who had a more doctrinaire approach, would take action unless companies were seen to do so (that is, Government legislation was a real possibility).[45] Although the CBI leadership was critical of the code, Cadbury won the support of the wider CBI membership at the CBI annual conference in early November.[46] Eventually, he won the debate with the CBI leadership over the need to report compliance with the code.[47]

The final version of the report appeared at the beginning of December 1992. This was similar to the draft report except that the final report responded to CBI concerns about the role of non-executives as policemen, by playing down the distinction between them and executive directors.[48] There was also an explicit distancing of the report from support for two-tier boards.[49] Though many had reservations about the report, there was widespread support in boardrooms and in the City. As one eminent City figure was quoted as saying, 'You can't be against, it you have to be for it.'[50] The media gave it a much more mixed reaction, ranging from a 'raspberry'[51] to 'an ambitious remit for self-regulation'.[52] The Government reaction was positive, with the Corporate Affairs Minister labelling it 'an authoritative statement of what needs to be done in a crucial area'.[53]

The general reaction in the City to the report was positive but several chief executives who were also chairmen were critical.[54] BTR's then chairman and CEO criticised the effect on the smooth operation of the board, given the clear role it gave to non-executives in monitoring executives.[55] The cost of implementation was estimated to be at least 10 per cent of the annual audit fee.[56]

The Stock Exchange quickly made it clear that it was not inclined to delist those companies who refused to implement the code.[57] Others pointed out that the report did not seem to pass the Maxwell test – preventing the collapse of another Maxwell Communications Corporation.[58] Some executives wanted mandatory backing for the report.[59] There was also a question as to whether the report had tackled the issue of poor internal control, which had been the trigger for it.[60]

The state of UK PLCs at the time of the Cadbury report was such that only eight FTSE100 companies complied with the main points of the code specifically:[61]

1. Separation of chairmen and chief executives
2. A majority of independent non-executive directors
3. An audit committee with a majority of non-executive directors
4. A remuneration committee with a majority of non-executive directors
5. A nomination committee with a majority of non-executive directors.

The report had set a deadline of 30 June 1993 for the beginning of reporting compliance with the code. By this time, 54 out of 66 reporting FTSE100 companies had complied with the reporting requirement.[62] The percentage of companies with a combined CEO and chairman of the board had declined from 25 per cent to 15 per cent. Within a year the percentage of FTSE350 companies with remuneration and audit committees had doubled and the percentage with nomination committees was rising.[63]

The committee continued to meet to monitor compliance with the code. It set up a working party to look at the area of internal controls in the company. This working party was under the chairmanship of Paul Rutteman, a technical partner at accountants Ernst and Young. This committee sought to devise guidelines on how a statement could be made on whether a company was a going concern and how it could define having an adequate system of internal control. This working party finally reported in December 1994, two years after the original report.[64]

The Cadbury Committee ceased in May 1995 when Sir Adrian bowed out with the presentation of a report on the implementation of the Cadbury Code. This report indicated an impressive change in boardroom behaviour.[65] Among FTSE250 companies, the percentage with an independent audit committee had risen from 45 per cent to 87 per cent; the percentage with a nomination committee had risen from 8 per cent to 60 per cent; the percentage with a remuneration committee had risen from 60 per cent to 98 per cent. Only seven companies had a combined chairman and chief executive with no named lead non-executive director as suggested by the code. The problem area for implementation was among the smallest 250 listed companies where, although compliance had risen sharply, there were still only a small minority of companies with independent audit or nomination committees.[66] There was also a problem of looking just at the letter rather than the spirit of recommendations.[67]

Many institutional investors and some parts of the media had noted that the original Cadbury Report had not addressed the issue of executive pay in great detail[68] (focusing instead on disclosure and transparency). In particular, the reporting of pay levels and the process for determining executive pay had not been discussed. Into 1994, this issue began to dominate the financial reports in the press on corporate governance. It was becoming clear that this was an issue that would have to be addressed.

The original report had specified that the issues of corporate governance should be re-examined by a successor committee to be set up no later than June 1995.[69] This was to give business a chance to implement the code and to consider its effects. The successor to the Cadbury Committee was to be the Hampel Committee.

Influences

We summarise and highlight the key influence groups on each stage of the process of the development of the Cadbury Committee in Table 2.1. *High* indicates significant influence, *Low* a small influence and *Medium* lies in between, – implies no measurable impact. Initial interest in corporate governance was wide-ranging against a background of recession (an exogenous factor). Financial stakeholders and the accounting and legal professions realised the business threat that poor internal

Table 2.1 Influences on the key stages in the development of the Cadbury Report

		Initial interest	Formation of committee	Terms of reference	Deliberation	Compilation	Presentation	Debate	Implementation
Business	Corporates	L	L	L	L	M	H	H	H
	Non-financial stakeholders	—	—	—	—	—	—	—	—
	Financial stakeholders	H	M	—	M	M	—	—	—
	Professionals	H	H	H	H	H	H	H	H
Authorities	Government	H	L	—	—	—	—	—	—
	Regulators	H	M	M	M	M	L	L	H
Public opinion	Media	H	L	L	—	M	H	H	—
	NGOs	—	—	—	—	—	—	—	—
	Popular feeling	H	—	—	—	—	—	—	—
Exogenous factors	Events	H	H	H	—	—	—	—	—

H = High, M = Medium, L = Low, — = None discernible.

control and board accountability caused (all were represented on the committee). The Government took an active interest in the issue, given the poor light it shed on the deregulated system that they wished to promote. This influence was exercised through encouragement from the Bank of England[70] at the time of the formation of the committee and the presence of a DTI representative on it. Adrian Cadbury had an excellent pedigree as a former company chairman, the head of the Bank of England's enterprise to promote non-executive directors (Pro-NED) and a member of the Court of the Bank of England. The Bank's influence on the committee also came through the presence of the Bank's advisor on corporate governance on the committee. Public interest and media attention on the well-publicised failures prompted the formation of the committee. There was only a low-key involvement of corporates in the initial phase, largely through Cadbury's own business background.

Professionals (and their regulators) dominated the formation of the committee, with the Financial Reporting Council taking the lead in recruiting members and in setting the terms of reference. Media interest waned as the investigation progressed. At the presentation of the findings, corporates were targeted in order to get them to buy into the findings. Their interests were robustly represented (by the CBI and vocal individual CEOs) in the subsequent debate and their acceptance of the recommendations was the key to successful implementation. The media followed the launch of the report and the subsequent debate around its recommendations, but interest waned over the long period between 1992 and 1995 when Cadbury himself made his valedictory report on implementation. The Stock Exchange's agreement to make it a listing requirement, that companies report on their degree of compliance with the code, was an essential element of regulatory promotion of the recommendations.

The Greenbury Committee and the issue of executive pay

As we noted above, it was recognised that a very specific issue that the Cadbury Report had not dealt with in great detail was that of the level (and rate of increase) of executive pay.[71] The Cadbury Report had recommended the establishment of a remuneration committee consisting wholly or mainly of non-executive directors, but the details of its policies had not been examined.[72] In the two years following the publication of the final report, this became a hot political issue, with newspapers highlighting three-year contracts, large perks and large pay increases.[73] Pension funds indicated that they wanted to see a greater link between pay and performance.[74] The Labour Party Opposition, assisted by the newspapers, highlighted the issue of 'fat cat' pay, particularly latching on to the large pay rises that many executives in privatised utilities received. Gordon Brown, then Labour's Treasury spokesman, highlighted the fact that utility privatisation had created 50 millionaires among executives, including all 14 of the chairmen of the regional electricity companies.[75] A rallying point became the 75 per cent pay rise announced in 1994 for the chairman of British Gas, Cedric Brown, who then became the target of a 'Cedric the Pig' campaign at the May 1995 British Gas AGM.[76] This campaign struck a nerve with the public at a time of relatively high unemployment and independent evidence that revealed that there was no discernible link between pay increases and company performance.[77] At the end of 1994, it was reckoned that £7 bn of a total of £10.5 bn of executive share options in listed UK companies did not relate to performance.[78]

The issue was highly embarrassing to the Government, which was already politically unpopular. Ministers were reportedly split on whether to approach the CBI to do something or to put pressure on shareholders to take action to punish underperformance.[79] The campaign on executive pay shed a rather poor light on one of their most spectacularly successful policies – utility privatisation – and led to embarrassment at perceived market excesses for a pro-business government. The Deputy Prime Minister Michael Heseltine, with responsibility for the presentation of Government policy, was concerned to distance the Government from the issue. He reportedly put pressure on the CBI to look into the matter and see if something could be done.[80] In public, he threatened legislation if business did not clean up its act.

Heseltine approached Richard Greenbury, Chairman of Marks & Spencer, to head a committee to look in to the issue of executive pay. The committee Greenbury formed had no formal sponsors, but was supported by the CBI, who provided for the secretarial and publication costs. The committee consisted of seven company chairmen, the head of the Institute of Directors, and two leading investment fund managers.[81] The committee sat for the first time in early 1995. The terms of reference were:

> To identify good practice in determining Directors' remuneration and prepare a Code of such practice for use by UK PLCs.
>
> (Greenbury Report, 1995, para 1.2, p. 9)

The committee met at Marks & Spencer's head offices and produced two draft reports before a final report was published in September 1995. The interim report had no specific criticism for the pay schemes at utilities – the issue that had led to its formation. However, this was corrected in the final report.[82] There was also a debate about whether executive pay should remain the prerogative of the board or should be the subject of a resolution at the AGM – an option which some of the investment organisations favoured.[83]

The final report's recommendations centred around new disclosure requirements and the functioning of the remuneration committee made up of non-executives who would determine both individual executive pay and pay policy.[84] Remuneration committee chairmen should be directly accountable to shareholders (rather than just the board).[85] There were recommendations on the elements of good policy which should be focused on the alignment of the interests of directors and shareholders. Remuneration committees were to give attention to incentivising long-term performance by avoiding issuing share options at a discount. Directors' service contracts should be a year or less. As with the Cadbury Report, enforcement was to be through a statement in the annual report by the remuneration committee which would explain any areas of non-compliance. Such a statement was to be a Stock Exchange listing requirement. Annual reports were also to carry details of each individual director's pay package rather than just those of the chairman and highest paid executive.

The reaction to the Greenbury Report was largely negative. The Labour Party announced that it was not satisfied with the report and that it would ban share options for all privatised utilities.[86] The toughness of the report was questioned because it allowed British Gas to claim that it was now at the leading edge of best practice, simply because it reported its policies.[87] There was also a debate about whether share options should be treated as income rather than as capital (and hence taxed more highly).[88] Both the CBI and IOD expressed worries that the report had not gone far enough in regulating business behaviour.[89] Corporates complained about the compliance burden that the new code placed on them.[90] Only the Government seemed satisfied,[91] perhaps because the committee had achieved its political purpose of deflecting a lot of the criticism away from it.

The issue of executive pay continued to rumble on long after the report. The Labour Party wrapped it up into the justification for their Windfall Tax on utilities plan which they enacted soon after coming to power in 1997. The issue of executive pay is regularly aired in the newspapers, as it has continued to rise faster than average earnings and to bear little relationship to the underlying performance of companies. If the intention of Greenbury was to make pay more responsive to performance, this seems to have failed. Indeed, it has been claimed that the large amount of information on pay which is available has encouraged pay rises, as comparisons of executive pay are now easier.[92] However, remuneration committees, in practice, do not appear to have much ability to influence pay, *per se*, as they rely on advisors to tell them what the 'going-rate' for a particular executive is. As one member of the committee puts it, 'the answer is obvious from the analysis of pay charts – to the nearest 1000 pounds'. Executive pay in the UK is determined largely by market forces (which may not be efficient), not by the nature of the corporate governance.[93]

In 1999, the Government initiated a follow-up consultation on directors' remuneration.[94] Following a lengthy consultation process by the DTI, in March 2001 the then Secretary of State for Trade and Industry, Stephen Byers, announced that the Government was planning to introduce secondary legislation to require quoted companies to publish a report on directors' remuneration in their annual report.[95] The legislation would specify that the contents of such a report would include individual directors' remuneration packages, the role of the board's remuneration committee, the board's remuneration policy and other disclosure requirements, including a company performance graph. The stated aim of this legal underpinning to the recommendations of the Greenbury Report was the desire to strengthen the link between boardroom pay and performance. In October 2001, the Government announced further that the new legislation on boardroom pay would also include a provision for an annual resolution to be put to shareholders on whether they accept the remuneration report.[96] Whether this will have any value in restraining directors' pay is highly questionable, given the immediate post-Greenbury experience.

Influences

The key influence groups at each stage of the process of development of the Greenbury Committee are summarised in Table 2.2. The table indicates the important initial roles for government, media, popular feeling and events. All of these influences reflected the fact that the privatisations of the 1990s gave rise to huge pay rises for the executives involved. British Gas was just one case. Indeed, it already complied with most of the recommendations of Greenbury before the report was published and had good corporate governance. However, the media were able to

Table 2.2 Influences on the key stages in the development of the Greenbury Report

		Initial interest	Formation of committee	Terms of reference	Deliberation	Compilation	Presentation	Debate	Implementation
Business	Corporates	L	H	H	H	H	H	H	H
	Non-financial stakeholders	H	L	L	L	L	L	L	L
	Financial stakeholders	L	H	H	H	H	H	H	H
	Professionals	—	—	—	—	—	—	—	—
Authorities	Government	H	H	H	H	H	H	H	H
	Regulators	—	—	—	—	—	—	—	M
Public opinion	Media	H	—	—	H	H	H	H	H
	NGOs	M	—	—	—	—	—	—	—
	Popular feeling	H	—	—	H	H	H	H	H
Exogenous factors	Events	H	—	—	—	—	—	—	—

H = High, M = Medium, L = Low, — = None discernible.

take such events and highlight them successfully because of genuine public concern about such pay rises.

The Government reacted to such events because of political reality. This led it to take the lead in the formation of the committee, with the help of the CBI and the company chairmen involved in the committee. Institutional investors were also significant, both on the committee, and in putting pressure on companies to reform. These groups continued to be significant through the process, with the Government threat of legislation promoting implementation and the rise of activist fund managers pushing for more revelation in annual accounts and asking questions of companies that did not comply. The regulators played no role until the implementation phase, when listing requirements of the Stock Exchange were invoked to enforce the code. Non-financial stakeholders, such as individuals as customers of utilities, play some role at the beginning of the process.[97]

Interestingly, the media and the public played no role in the formation of the committee or in the setting of its terms of reference. Greenbury had a poor relationship with the media [98] and the committee was made up of senior executives and did not consult with the media or the wider public. The composition of the committee and its inadequate interaction with the media during the whole process undoubtedly contributed to the poor media reception of the report. Given the nature of the issue, which meant that the problem was largely intractable, the committee would have done well to involve more of its critics in its deliberations in order to achieve more of a public consensus on the issue. The benefits for the business community of doing this are illustrated in the case of the Company Law Review.

The Hampel Committee, or Cadbury II

The Hampel Committee started life in a paragraph[99] of the Cadbury Report that specified that the code on corporate governance was to be reviewed after three years. By 1995, the Cadbury Report, in spite of earlier disquiet, had been widely accepted and was viewed as having brought about significant and worthwhile changes in behaviour.[100] Only a few of the more maverick FTSE100 chairmen continued to speak out against it, mainly from those few companies which continued to combine the role of chairman and chief executive in the person of a long-standing powerful individual.[101] The Chairman of the Financial Reporting Council, which had been instrumental in setting up the Cadbury Committee, announced in April 1995 that there would be a review.[102] However, the media comment on corporate governance continued to highlight the issue of executive pay. Towards the later part of the year, it emerged that two prospective chairmen had been approached but, in the light of the difficulties Sir Richard Greenbury was experiencing, had turned down the opportunity to head 'Cadbury II'.[103] Eventually, in November, Sir Ronnie Hampel, then chairman of ICI, was announced as head of the committee.[104]

The committee was established with the support of London Stock Exchange, the CBI, the IOD, the Consultative Committee of the Accountancy Bodies, the National Association of Pension Funds and the Association of British Insurers. Representatives of each of these organisations were approached to be on the committee.[105] The involvement of the investment community comprising insurance and pension fund representatives was a notable addition to the range of backgrounds present on the original Cadbury committee and reflected the importance of the investment community in ensuring good governance.[106]

The committee's terms of reference were:

> to promote high standards of Corporate governance in the interests of investor protection and in order to preserve and enhance the standing of companies listed on the Stock Exchange. The committee's remit will extend to listed companies only. Against this background the committee will:
>
> (a) conduct a review of the Cadbury code and its implementation to ensure that the original purpose is being achieved, proposing amendments to and deletions from the code as necessary;
> (b) keep under review the role of directors, executive and non-executive, recognising the need for board cohesion and the common legal responsibilities of all directors;
> (c) be prepared to pursue any relevant matters arising from the report of the Study Group on Directors' Remuneration chaired by Sir Richard Greenbury;
> (d) address as necessary the role of shareholders in corporate governance issues;
> (e) address as necessary the role of auditors in corporate governance issues; and
> (f) deal with any other relevant matters.
>
> Without impairing investor protection the committee will always keep in mind the need to restrict the regulatory burden on companies, e.g. by substituting principles for detail wherever possible.
>
> (Hampel Report, 1998, Annex, p. 66)

The first meeting of the committee did not take place until the end of January 1996.[107] The Government was very unpopular and the Labour Party was continuing to campaign against executive pay and windfall profits from utilities. Labour made it clear that it expected the Hampel Committee to provide some clear leadership in the area of governance, or else it would act in Government.[108] A draft Labour Party manifesto in June 1996 made it clear that legislation would wait for the outcome of the report.[109] There was also a suggestion that the Labour Party might establish an expert panel on corporate governance.[110] From the beginning, however, Hampel made it clear that he was not a radical and that radical changes were unlikely to be recommended by the committee.[111]

The committee met in ICI's offices and received many submissions on the subject of governance.[112] This delayed the publication of a draft report until August 1997.[113] In this draft, the committee emphasised the need to get back to establishing good principles of governance before codes. The City was relieved that the report favoured no more radical reform and that the momentum for more corporate governance had been stopped.[114] Hampel's recommendations endorsed Cadbury's original report but did not significantly seek to strengthen it. The reaction to the draft was decidedly mixed.[115] Hermes, the independent activist fund manager, thought that it had not clarified the role of an independent director.[116] The IOD wanted more direction on what long-term incentive packages should be offered to executives.[117] The Industry Secretary, Margaret Beckett, speaking at the CBI conference, indicated that the Labour Party (now in Government) considered that both corporate governance and company law should be beefed up.[118] The labour unions were concerned that nothing was being done to address short-termism towards investment in the UK.[119] Hampel expressed himself concerned about the negative reaction to the draft report and there were fears that report would not go far enough to divert legislation.[120]

The final report was published towards the end of January 1998. The principal recommendations were that companies should include in their annual accounts a narrative statement of how they apply 'the relevant principles' to their particular circumstances. The principles highlighted were: that chairman and chief executive should be separated and if not, this should be explained; there should be a balance between non-executive and executive directors; nomination committees, recommended by Cadbury, should be recognised as good practice; and that all directors should submit themselves to regular re-election. A lead non-executive director should be identified through whom concerns could be raised if there was no separation of chair and chief executive.

The Hampel Report stated that individual directors should not take part in decisions on their own remuneration package. Remuneration policy should remain a matter for the board.[121] The board should maintain a sound system of internal control, though it was not specified how it should do this. Hampel supported the recommendations of Cadbury that audit committees should be made up of non-executive directors. Overall, the report can be seen as endorsing Cadbury while not recommending anything new, such as allowing shareholders to vote on executive pay packages.

Having been widely discussed at the draft stage, there was limited reaction to the publication of the final report. However, the day after the publication, Margaret Beckett announced that there would be a widespread review of company law.[122] This provoked some pleas from the City that self-regulation should be given time to work and that the review should not be too wide-ranging.[123] However, the Hampel Report was widely seen as letting business off lightly.[124]

A combined code, drawing together the Cadbury, Greenbury and Hampel recommendations, was published by the London Stock Exchange in June 1998.[125]

By 1998, the UK was widely recognised as leading the world in the area of corporate governance.[126] The Cadbury Report had had time to filter through the leading companies in the UK and several other countries had initiated similar reviews of their corporate governance and come to similar conclusions, inspired by the Cadbury Report. However, considered comment pointed out that governance reforms had made little difference to executive pay and that reforms still did not pass the Maxwell test.[127] Governance was not crucial to performance, with evidence continuing to suggest that more non-executives on a board did not improve performance and that companies combining chief executive and chairman tended to do better. The evidence was that governance was not the crucial determinant of performance and that self-regulation could go only so far in improving underlying competitiveness.[128]

Influences

The key influences in the development of the Hampel Report are outlined in Table 2.3. The Hampel Report was foreseen in the Cadbury Report and the Financial Reporting Council, representing the accountancy profession and the Stock Exchange, was the institution that ensured the carrying out of the Cadbury recommendation. The key role of the accountancy profession in auditing governance statements might explain why professionals were keen to re-examine the issue and, if possible,

Table 2.3 Influences on the key stages in the development of the Hampel Report

		Initial interest	Formation of committee	Terms of reference	Deliberation	Compilation	Presentation	Debate	Implementation
Business	Corporates	L	M	M	M	M	M	L	L
	Non-financial stakeholders	L	L	L	L	L	L	L	L
	Financial stakeholders	M	H	M	M	M	M	L	L
	Professionals	H	H	H	H	H	H	H	H
Authorities	Government	L	—	M	L	L	L	H	L
	Regulators	H	H	H	—	—	—	L	H
Public opinion	Media	L	L	L	L	L	L	L	L
	NGOs	L	L	L	L	L	L	L	L
	Popular feeling	L	—	—	—	—	—	—	—
Exogenous factors	Events	L	—	—	—	—	—	—	—

H = High, M = Medium, L = Low, — = None discernible.

promote the corporate governance industry. Given the wide-ranging and initially uncomfortable adjustment following Cadbury, corporates had little interest in further reform and other non-financial stakeholders had no particular interest.

However, corporates were well represented on the committee, especially in the person of the chairman. Financial stakeholders were significantly represented in pushing for further debate on the accountability of boards to shareholders and on the committee itself. The Government had little influence, in contrast to Greenbury, except in that terms of reference reflected concerns about possible legislation. The media, NGOs, popular feeling and events played little role. The report appears to have been little influenced by the threat of Government action, though this was very real. This may have been because as the economy recovered and rate of bankruptcies fell, corporate governance *per se*, as opposed to the levels of executive pay in particular, was not a matter for political concern. The increasingly pro-business stance of the 'New' Labour Party and the lack of public identification with the issues may have meant that the threat of legislation was largely seen as an empty one. The Hampel Report may not have been so significant in itself, but it did, however, seem to coincide closely with the Government's call for a fundamental review of Company Law.

The Turnbull Committee and internal control – tying up unfinished business

The initial impetus to set up the Cadbury Committee had arisen because of a lack of adequate internal control systems within the high-profile corporate failures in the late 1980s. A well functioning internal control system should 'facilitate [a company's] effective and efficient operation by enabling it to respond to ... risks. This includes the safeguarding of assets from inappropriate use or from loss and fraud, and ensuring that liabilities are identified and managed'.[129] Internal control systems do this by providing for appropriate oversight of financial transactions undertaken by the company through the specification of authority structures, appropriate information and communication processes and a capacity to review the ongoing effectiveness of internal control arrangements.

Although the Cadbury Report did discuss the need for effective internal control, that did not turn out to be its main focus. It delegated a detailed review of internal control to a successor committee. This turned out to be the Rutteman Committee, which eventually published a long report in 1994. The Rutteman Report received quite limited coverage and was not widely perceived as having closed the matter of appropriate internal-control systems in UK corporate governance. The Hampel Report reiterated the need for a sound system of internal financial control. However, there was no guidance on what the system should look like apart from the requirement that the need for an internal-audit function should be reviewed regularly if it did not exist.[130]

The Institute for Chartered Accountants in England and Wales (ICEAW) and the Stock Exchange discussed the need for more detailed guidance following the publication of the Hampel Report. They drew up the terms of reference for a new governance committee that was to conclude the work that the Cadbury Committee had started. The committee was sponsored by the ICAEW and chaired by Nigel Turnbull, then Chief Financial Officer of Rank Group plc and also Chairman of the Technical Committee of the 100 Group of leading UK companies. The Institute took the lead in suggesting names to the Stock Exchange of who should be on the committee.

The Turnbull Report intended to:

> reflect sound business practice whereby internal control is embedded in the business processes by which a company pursues its objectives; remain relevant over time in the continually evolving business environment; and enable each company to apply it in a manner which takes account of its particular circumstances.
>
> (Turnbull Report, 1999, para. 8, p. 4)

The first meeting took place in late autumn 1998 and the committee met monthly until April 1999. The members of the committee were mostly trained accountants and were quickly able to produce an interim report in April 1999.[131] The earlier Rutteman Report had concluded that it was not possible to specify how to improve internal control, but just internal financial control. The Rutteman Report was technical and compliance with it was specified by the Stock Exchange as an interim target. However, the Turnbull Report attempted to remain more general and go back to first principles on how to make sure risk management was embedded within the system of the company. The Turnbull Report recommendations superseded the Rutteman guidance.[132]

The final report was published in September 1999 and specified the elements of a sound system of internal control, the process for reviewing effectiveness of internal control procedures, the need for a board statement on internal control, and discussed the appropriateness of having an internal-audit function. It concluded that the elements of a sound system of internal control should be embedded within the operations of a company, form part of its culture, be capable of quick response to evolving risks and include well-specified procedures for reporting warning signs. The process for reviewing effectiveness should be well defined, involving continuous monitoring and annual assessment. The annual board statement on internal control should include a statement on how the company had applied the Turnbull code principles, state that there was a process in place, summarise the process that it had used to review effectiveness and not make any disclosures that were misleading. Companies were recommended to have an internal-audit function. However, where they did not have one, there should be an annual review of the decision not to and disclosure in the annual report about the presence or absence of an annual review of this decision.

The Turnbull Report was short and to the point and generally perceived as having completed the work left unfinished by Hampel in this area.[133] The reaction to the report was positive, with business accepting its practical recommendations. The report was seen to be timely as 58 per cent of businesses surveyed wanted to improve their system of internal control.[134] The precise nature of the recommendations means that it is likely that they may quietly have far-reaching effects in reducing the likelihood of the sort of scandals that promoted the ten-year review of corporate governance in the UK.[135]

Influences

The main influences on the Turnbull Report are outlined in Table 2.4. Events had some influence on the setting up of the committee, through the drivers behind the Cadbury Report, the perceived narrowness of the subsequent Rutteman Report and the unfinished business in the Hampel Report. The Stock Exchange (the regulator) and accountancy profession were the main actors behind the need to complete the work on reforming this aspect of corporate governance. To some extent, corporates wanted guidance and financial institutions saw the need for guidance (there was a representative from the pensions industry on the committee).

The committee was mainly made up of representatives who were members of the accountancy profession (eight out of ten members).[136] This reflected the perceived technical nature of the issue and this clearly had a big influence on the final recommendations. The Hampel Committee invited a significant amount of interest at the outset and during its deliberations but there was no discernible media or public interest in the development of the Turnbull Committee and no Government influence over it. Corporates were involved in the debate over the interim

Table 2.4 Influences on the key stages in the development of the Turnbull Report

		Initial interest	Formation of committee	Terms of reference	Deliberation	Compilation	Presentation	Debate	Implementation
Business	Corporates	L	L	—	—	—	—	M	H
	Non-financial stakeholders	—	—	—	—	—	—	—	—
	Financial stakeholders	L	L	—	—	—	—	—	—
	Professionals	H	H	H	H	H	H	H	H
Authorities	Government	—	—	—	—	—	—	—	H
	Regulators	H	H	H	—	—	—	H	H
Public opinion	Media	—	—	—	—	—	M	—	—
	NGOs	—	—	—	—	—	—	—	—
	Popular feeling	—	—	—	—	—	—	—	—
Exogenous factors	Events	M	—	—	—	—	—	—	—

H = High, M = Medium, L = Low, — = None discernible.

report and were important in accepting and implementing the recommendations of the report. Once again, the incorporation of reporting requirements into listing rules by the Stock Exchange was an important driver of implementation. The report was drafted by the staff members from the ICAEW on the committee and the presentation of the report was led by Turnbull himself.

It is interesting to note that Government and private sector interest in corporate governance begins to diverge ahead of the Turnbull Report. The Government initiated the Company Law Review shortly after the publication of the Hampel Report. This review continues to examine the big picture of what companies are for in a modern economy, while the private sector focuses on filling in some of the details missed in its earlier reports.

The Company Law Review: the Government considers active intervention in corporate governance

The election of a Labour Government in May 1997 signalled the end of the 18-year era of strongly pro-business and largely *laissez-faire* Conservative administrations in the UK. In Opposition, the Labour Party had been critical of the Government for inaction on the issue of executive pay and critical of the lack of progress which private-sector-led governance initiatives had achieved. The new administration's first Secretary of State for Trade and Industry, Margaret Beckett, was open to the possibility of government legislation should the Hampel Report fall short of what the Government wanted.[137] Following the publication of the Hampel Report in January 1998, Mrs Beckett announced a wholesale review of company law in March 1998.

Company law covers many pieces of legislation relating to the behaviour of companies and their directors (*see* DTI, 1998). The most important current Act is the *Companies Act* of 1985 which consolidates previous legislation. However, many of the key principles in this Act are based on the *Joint Stock Companies Act* of 1844 and the *Limited Liability Act* of 1855. Since these formative pieces of legislation, there have been major consolidations of the law in 1908, 1929, 1948. The last major review took place under the Jenkins Committee, which sat from 1960–62. Thus a pattern of major review every twenty or so years was established. By 1997, company law was generally considered to be well overdue for such a review in the light of Britain's entry into the EU and legal developments around the world. The Government identified a number of issues in need of attention in the current legislation: over-formal language;

excessive detail; over-regulation; complex structure; and obsolescent provisions.[138]

However, there was also the issue of corporate governance. The introduction to the Company Law Review acknowledged the contribution of the Cadbury, Greenbury and Hampel Reports and that 'the issues dealt with under the new (Combined) Code are more suitable for best practice than legislation'.[139] However, it was noted that 'there may however be a need for legislation in certain areas which are not covered by the new Code, or where experience shows that some legal underpinning is needed.'[140] Some of the example areas for investigation are: the duties of directors (in particular whether shareholders should have a duty to take other stakeholders' views into account in addition to shareholders), the conduct of AGMs (to encourage shareholder resolutions and voting) and shareholder control over executive pay (in order to keep executive pay rises down). We note that all of these areas were heavily debated in the light of earlier recommendations. Thus, while the motivation for the process known as the Company Law Review was not primarily driven by the perceived failure of private sector governance initiatives, there is no doubt that the timing of the Company Law Review (immediately following Hampel) and its scope were influenced by the earlier governance reports.

Thus, the terms of reference for the Company Law Review are: to consider how core company law can be modernised, to consider whether enough legal vehicles exist for business at all levels, to consider the proper relationship between company law and non-statutory standards of corporate behaviour, to review the extent to which foreign companies operating in the UK should be regulated under British law and to make recommendations accordingly.[141]

The motivation for the Company Law Review has come from the Government, strongly influenced by the Law Society. The Company Law Review has been conducted by a steering group and associated working groups. The steering group has been responsible for overseeing the process and this met once a month between 1998 and mid-2001. Working groups were chaired by members of the steering group and met as often as bi-weekly. The steering group was chaired by a civil servant from the DTI. The whole process has been overseen by a senior official appointed by the DTI, who also sat on each of the working groups. The review has been as inclusive as possible, with a further consultative committee reviewing the work of the other groups. The steering group has also been responsible for producing a number of consultation documents which have taken the process forward so far.

The steering group consisted of a broad mix of people including academic lawyers, practising lawyers, company executives, economists and one journalist.[142] It worked on the basis of consensus.

The steering group has produced four major documents, in February 1999, March 2000, November 2000 and July 2001, which develop the overall framework, and a number of other papers relating to specific aspects of the law such as company formation and law concerning overseas companies.[143] The final main report (DTI, 2001) includes proposals for an inclusive statement of directors' duties, which would require directors to take into account the implications for the company over time and wider relationships, such as those with employees, suppliers, customers and the community in general. The report also proposes an operating and financial review that would allow for greater transparency for public companies and large private companies. The hope is that this will encourage an increase in transparency in the corporate sector and raise the standard of corporate reporting generally (*see* Parkinson, 2002). The report steers clear of the issue of executive pay, as this was the responsibility of a separate consultation. The report has restated a commitment to preserving the 'comply or explain' approach of the Combined Code rather than converting parts of the Code into substantive requirements.[144]

Margaret Beckett moved from Trade and Industry in mid-1998, soon after the launch of the Company Law Review. Between then and July 2001, three more pro-business ministers have held the post and the issue of the Company Law Review seems to have left the news agenda.[145] There was little reporting of the various stages of the review in the media. The little reporting that there was highlighted the unions' continuing concern that the issue of executive pay should be addressed[146] and concerns on the part of the business community that the review might be used to promote the stakeholder approach.[147] The publication of the final main report of the steering group was launched by the Government in July 2001 to meet with general approval of interested groups, such as the unions, and the accountancy and legal professions.[148] In early 2002, the Government was considering how to respond to the steering group's final report with a view to bringing forward a new *Companies Act* in 2003.

The issue of corporate governance is much less political than it was ten years ago, with the economy enjoying steady economic growth and corporate failures at a low level. It may be that it will take a fresh recession and/or a new set of corporate scandals to reveal sufficient weaknesses in the system of corporate governance to prompt further radical re-examination in either the public or private sectors.

Table 2.5 Influences on the key stages in the development of the Company Law Review

		Initial interest	Formation of committee	Terms of reference	Deliberation	Compilation	Presentation	Debate	Implementation
Business	Corporates	L	L	L	L	L	L	—	—
	Non-financial stakeholders	H	H	H	H	H	L	—	—
	Financial stakeholders	M	M	M	M	M	L	—	—
	Professionals	H	H	H	H	H	H	—	—
Authorities	Government	H	H	M	L	L	H	—	—
	Regulators	—	—	—	—	—	—	—	—
Public opinion	Media	L	L	L	—	—	L	—	—
	NGOs	M	M	M	M	M	L	—	—
	Popular feeling	L	L	L	—	—	—	—	—
Exogenous factors	Events	—	—	—	—	—	—	—	—

H = High, M = Medium, L = Low, — = None discernible.

Influences

The influences on the development of the Company Law Review are summarised in Table 2.5. Although it is not possible to comment on the last two stages of the process, which have yet to be completed, it is possible to comment on the other stages. Business has had a considerable input into the process, mainly via the legal profession with additional influences from non-financial stakeholders, such as trade unions concerned about the impacts of merger decisions on jobs. Financial stakeholders have had some influence through direct input into the process. The direct influence of corporates, especially through their representative trade organisations, has been limited.

The Government was the prime influence group in setting up the review process but has gradually withdrawn its direct influence as the process has progressed, such that the deliberation and compilation of the report are the responsibility of the steering group and working groups. However, it retained some influence through the DTI oversight of the process. Public opinion operating through the media and popular opinion has tailed away (from an initially low level) as the review has progressed. The decline in the interest of these two groups would seem to be an explanatory factor in the decline of Government interest (although the Government is committed to a new *Companies Act*). NGOs have retained a significant degree of interest in the process, given that many of the provisions relate to them, and they have been involved in the consultation group. The healthy economy throughout the process has ensured that there have been no significant exogenous factors influencing the process. In contrast to the other investigations into governance, there has been no role for the Stock Exchange and no formal involvement from the accountancy profession.

Detailed Conclusions

We summarise our main findings on the influences on the corporate governance debates in the UK in Table 2.6. This table highlights the nature of the issue involved and the relative influence of the different groups on the process, and offers an overall assessment of the process based on our perceptions informed by the media and academic comment. On the basis of this comparison and the earlier Tables 2.1–5, we discuss a number of conclusions in the remainder of this chapter.

Table 2.6 Summary assessment of influences on the different governance debates in the UK

	Nature of issues	Influences					Overall assessment	
		Business community	Authorities	Public opinion	Exogenous factors	Quality of process	Impact of process on outcome	
Cadbury	Specific – related to high profile failure	Varied	High	Initially high	High – economy unfavourable	Very high	Very high – visionary	
Greenbury	Specific – related to cases	High	High	High	High – Cedric Brown's pay rise	Very poor	High – inconclusive	
Hampel	General – revisiting Cadbury	Varied	Low	Low	Low – economy favourable	Initially medium, later improved	High – low key outcome	
Turnbull	Technical – of professional concern	Varied	Low	Low	Low	Focused and efficient	Very high – professional	
Company Law Review	General – motivated political views in opposition	Varied	High at official level, declining at political level	Varied – linked to Greenbury initially	Low	Consultation comprehensive	Very high – unlikely to be radical	

1. Corporate governance topics attract different levels of public, political or media interest.   In general, corporate governance is an abstract, technical subject which is consequently neither well understood nor of great interest to the public, politicians or the media. However, the corporate-governance issue can attract much higher levels of attention as a result of being associated with other issues of public interest. In this case, the issue is not really of importance in itself but because of the wider issues it reminds people about.

Table 2.6 shows that only the issue of executive pay and the associated Greenbury Report has attracted sustained public interest. This is perhaps because executive pay resonates with many wider issues, such as the impact of Thatcherite policies on the economy through privatisation. It raises some the fundamental issues of the benefits of the free market as opposed to a more egalitarian socialist economy. The more general issue of corporate responsibility raised by the Company Law Review does not so obviously link to politically charged debates and so initial political interest in the absence of obvious electoral advantage in the issue has not been sustained.

2. The process of addressing issues of corporate governance has significantly influenced the outcome of the individual reports.   It seems very likely that the process of addressing the issue of corporate governance in the UK has significantly influenced the outcome.

Table 2.6 illustrates the links between the conduct of the process on the outcome. The Cadbury Committee did an excellent job because it had a visionary leader who had an enormous influence on the outcome and did a lot of work to debate the issues. The Greenbury Report did little to deal with the issue of executive pay rises because it consisted of senior executives who benefited from the status quo and hence were unlikely to propose radical changes or provide a convincing endorsement for the status quo. The Turnbull Report was focused and business-like, and had a well-defined professional task. The Company Law Review has been very inclusive but, for that reason, is unlikely to lead to radical legislation.

3. Corporate influences on the process and content of the reports have been surprisingly weak.   The natural assumption would be that because corporations are most affected by the results of corporate governance enquiries, then they would also seek to exert the most influence on the process and content.

In fact, companies have had little influence on the early, formative stages in the enquiries of Cadbury, Hampel, Turnbull, or the Company Law Review. Nor are their representatives, the CBI and the IOD very influential, despite what are probably very considerable efforts to reach opinion on corporate governance and related issues.

Corporate interests were probably most clearly taken account of through the person of Adrian Cadbury as a company chairman and industrialist. His report was governed by a concern to find solutions which companies could adopt and by which they could change their behaviour. It was the pragmatic enquiry of an industrialist. The irony is that Cadbury was not chosen as a result of his association with business interests, but because of his connections with financial interests. He had been a member of the Court of the Bank of England and was Chairman of the Bank sponsored Pro-NED.

The Greenbury Committee did have significant representation from company chairmen. However, there was corporate interest only because the government was pressing it hard in the light of public opinion. This committee was a response to very visible outside pressure and did not arise because of a corporate desire to shape the debate.

4. The influence of non-governmental bodies and non-financial stakeholders on the process and content of the enquiries has been very weak. Lobby groups representing non-financial stakeholders (for instance, trade unions and consumer groups) and NGOs might have been expected to have had a significant influence on the debate, given the stakeholder debate (*see* Hutton, 1995) that has been carried on in and around the debate about corporate governance. These groups are vocal and politically influential.

However, our research has not detected much direct influence. The governance committees show no representation from these groups and little discernible influence on the process or the outcome. There has been some involvement of these groups in the Company Law Review but it seems likely that the very fact of including them in the process is merely to reduce their ability to criticise the outcome. The language of stakeholding has been very much toned down by the Labour Government as time has progressed and the consequences of the Company Law Review seem unlikely to be particularly radical in increasing the influence of non-financial stakeholders in the boardroom.

5. Institutional investors have had much less influence on the process and content of the enquiries than might have been expected. One might argue that institutional investors, who stand to lose from poor corporate governance leading to mismanagement and fraud, have a significant interest in corporate governance. Much of the emphasis in corporate governance has been on improving the quality of published information on companies available to market participants. Investors depend on receiving accurate information so that the price represents an effective measure of the value of a firm. Institutional investors have been the subject of a separate set of investigations and consultations initiated by the first Myners Report in 1996.[149] Indeed, Adrian Cadbury recently suggested that the focus in corporate governance should now shift to an examination of their role.[150]

Our research seems to indicate that institutional investors (or financial stakeholders in Table 2.6) have had a rather patchy influence. There was some influence on the setting up of the Cadbury and Hampel committees but very little in the case of Greenbury and Hampel. Institutional investors have been concerned only with the Company Law Review (at the Government's invitation) and Turnbull to a limited extent. This probably reflects the lack of activism among the investment community in the UK and it is notable that it is the activist funds, such as Hermes, that have made most contribution to the debate.

6. Professionals have had a significant influence on the process and content of the corporate governance debates.   Corporate governance has long been viewed as a technical subject concerned with the robustness and reliability of corporate auditing systems. This implies that professionals such as accountants and lawyers are likely to be heavily involved in the practice of corporate governance and in debates about its reform. Bad corporate governance threatens the integrity of such governance professionals, in terms of the public reputation, and in terms of professional liability (Robert Maxwell's auditors did pay compensation). The ICAEW and the Law Society are well resourced and highly effective. We would, therefore, expect these professional bodies to be keen to influence the governance debate.

Our analysis suggests that accountants were a driving force behind the setting up of Cadbury, they had an influence on the terms of reference and were well represented on the committee. Similarly, there were accountants on the Hampel Committee and on the Company Law Review. The trend in UK corporate governance towards a greater evidence on measurement, audit and reporting undoubtedly reflects the influence of accountants on the process of corporate governance. It remains to be seen whether this will serve British industry well or whether it will act to reduce innovation and entrepreneurship.

7. Political influences on the process and content of the enquiries have been variable.   Corporate governance is about the executive power at the heart of capitalism. As such, we would expect there to be a significant degree of political interest and influence. It is potentially an area where political influence can be brought to bear at minimal fiscal cost.

However, parliamentary time is scarce, the business lobby powerful and corporate governance is not usually a vote winning issue. Thus, the expectation of political involvement would be a contingent one: where the corporate governance resonates with wider issues, then there will be political influence, but where it does not there will be little political interest.

The evidence in Table 2.6 is broadly in line with this argument. Executive pay was a burning issue for the Government and touched on a number of Government policies on privatisation, entrepreneurship and tax, where the Government was criticised. The Government were most active in the case of the Greenbury Report (and the whole issue of directors' pay) but their influence has been much more muted in the case of the other reports. The lack of sustained political interest in corporate governance is illustrated by the low profile nature of the Company Law Review.

8. Financial regulators have had a significant influence. Failures in financial reporting triggered the initial interest in corporate governance since 1990. As such, it might be expected that financial regulators such as the Financial Reporting Council, the Bank of England, the Stock Exchange and later the Financial Services Authority would have a concern to ensure appropriate steps were taken to improve financial reporting.

Corporate governance was initially promoted by the Bank of England, which was very influential in the formation of the Cadbury Committee. They perceived that the integrity of the market system was at stake if financial reporting was inadequate. The Bank of England subsequently withdrew from the area of corporate governance, with the privatisation of Pro-NED.[151] The Stock Exchange, in spite of suggestions that it might reduce its involvement, has continued to be very influential in the formation of subsequent committees and through their underpinning of reform through the listing rules. If volunteerism has been effective in the UK, it is because of the significance of the Stock Exchange in the UK economy and the power of the Stock Exchange required reporting requirements to force companies to justify their systems of corporate governance. The Financial Reporting Council, as a regulator of financial reporting, has acted as the sponsor of the Cadbury and Hampel Reports.

9. Media influence on the process and content of the enquiry has been patchy. One view of the media is that they create issues. Another is that they pick up issues which public opinion is concerned about. In the first case, the issue is likely to die if public opinion is not interested in it.

The evidence is that the media were powerful in recognising the debate when there was an event or public issue for it to expose. Thus, it featured the scandals that led to setting up Cadbury and cases of excessive executive pay that provided the background to the Greenbury Committee. Where there was no event or public issue, as was the case with Hampel and Turnbull, the media seem to have had little impact on the debate (Table 2.6).

Interestingly, even though the stakeholder argument is one that interests the media, the media were not a trigger for the setting up of the Company Law Review.

Some of the committees were better at handling the media than others. Cadbury worked closely with the press, as did Hampel. This paid off in terms of constructive coverage of the debates and of the final report. By contrast, Greenbury seems to have made no secret of his dislike for the press and this does not appear to have helped the media reaction to his report. It is, however, not clear that a more robust engagement with the press about the difficulty of the issue of executive pay would have led to a better media reaction to the publication and a reduction in public disquiet about the way executive pay was set.

10. Events have been sufficient but not necessary conditions for governance reviews. When asked what influenced politics, Harold Macmillan famously replied: 'Events dear boy, events'. We might, therefore, expect that events that raise strong public interest in corporate governance, such as business failures, shape the conduct and findings of the enquiry set up to deal with the event. The conclusion is that events are not a necessary condition for an enquiry, but can be a sufficient one.

The conduct and conclusions of the Cadbury Report would support this hypothesis. The composition of the committee, the financial and structural nature of the solution reflects its origins in creative accounting and the failure of companies within six months of a clear audit. The Greenbury Committee was also a creature of events. Turnbull, Hampel and the Company Law Review are not, except in the weak sense that they were the outcome of the earlier committees.

11. Macro-economic conditions have influenced the development of the debate. It could be expected that the state of the economy has a significant influence on the approach to corporate governance. In a recession, there is greater fear of company failure, the public feel-good factor is weaker and executives under pressure to produce results are open to the temptation to misreporting. In a recession, low performers are revealed for what they are and are no longer disguised by the buoyancy of the economy.

The pattern of macro-economic growth since 1990 tends to support this view. Many of the corporate excesses of the 1980s that led to the dramatic failures which stimulated the Cadbury Committee were exposed when the economy moved into recession. The principal interest in corporate governance in the UK has been when the economy was in recession in 1989–92. Cadbury recommended the most radical changes to the UK system of corporate governance. Since then, outside interest has diminished during the subsequent long boom. This has reduced the pressure for further radical change, as evidenced by the less significant conclusions of subsequent committees.

12. Business has retained control of the governance debate since 1990. The debate on corporate governance was initiated in 1990 by business itself in an attempt to head off interference from government. In spite of the claims of some that self-regulation was not going to be a permanent solution following the Cadbury Report,[152] this has proved to be the case so far. Though there have been periodic threats of fundamental reform, this is not likely to be initiated in the near future. As Morris puts it, 'if the Government can avoid legislating, it will owe much to the public relations efforts of Cadbury, Greenbury, Tim Melville Ross (IoD), and every other great and good member of the "something must be done" chorus; at the very least they have proved the City's willingness to respond to public anxiety and media criticism.'[153] The Government's recent proposals for legislating on directors' remuneration are hardly radical and seem unlikely to have much restraining effect.

Table 2.6 clearly shows that business has had the most significant influence in the four governance committees. It seems likely to have exerted a large influence on the conduct of the Company Law Review through the constitution of the steering group and through the general influence of business on the Labour Party, which ensures that radical changes in corporate governance in the absence of obvious electoral advantage – represented by media and public pressure – are unlikely to happen in the foreseeable future.

Notes

1 Cadbury Report (1992, para. 2.5, p. 15). This is quite a narrow definition. By contrast, Turnbull (1997, p. 181) suggests a much broader definition: 'Corporate governance describes all the influences affecting the institutional processes, including those for appointing the controllers and/or regulators, involved in organizing the production and sale of goods and services. Described in this way, corporate governance includes all types of firms whether or not they are incorporated into law.'

2 *See* Charkham, 1994 and Stock *et al.*, 1999.

3 *See,* for example, Franks and Mayer (1990).

4   *See www.dti.gov.uk/cld/review.htm*

5   *See* Davis Global Advisors Inc (2000) *Leading Corporate Governance Indicators*, p. 4, available from *www.davisglobal.com/publications/lcgi/lcgi_execsumm.pdf* This shows that the UK is the leading country in terms of corporate governance for 1996–2000 among seven of the world's top developed nations, including the US and Japan. This is interesting because many of suggestions for the improvement of UK corporate governance were around before the 1990s, *see* Bob Tricker, 'Corporate Governance II – Building Better Boards, *Director*, February 1987, vol. 40, issue 7, pp. 53–4, for example.

6   *See*, for example, the beginning of the Cadbury Report which states ' ... the effectiveness with which ... boards discharge their responsibilities determines Britain's competitive position'. (Cadbury Report, 1992, para. 1.1, p. 11).

7   Jones and Pollitt (1998, p. 5).

8   For a good review of the background to the Cadbury Report, *see* Boyd (1996); for a review of the governance debate, *see* Cadbury (2000); for evidence on the effects of particular governance structures, *see* Cook and Deakin (1999); for comment on the Company Law Review, *see* Monks (2000); for a view of an alternative system, *see* Kay and Silbertson (1995).

9   *www.cbi.org.uk/*

10   *www.iod.co.uk/*

11   *www.abi.org.uk/*

12   *www.napf.co.uk/*

13   *www.icaew.co.uk/*

14   *www.lawsociety.org.uk/*

15   *www.fsa.gov.uk/*

16   *www.londonstockexchange.com/*

17   *www.frc.org.uk/*

18   This is the World Bank definition. *See http://wbln0018.worldbank.org/essd/ess d.nsf/NGOs/Home*

19   *www.pirc.co.uk/*

20   For timely support for this view, *see* 'Leading Article: The Guinness Verdict', *Financial Times*, 28 August 1990, p. 16.

21   OECD (1991).

22   *See* Jones and Pollitt (1996) for some background material.

23   *See* Tony Gray, 'City View: Regulation clearly a massive failure', *Lloyd's List*, 12 December 1991, p. 5.

24   For an articulation of this view, *see* Hutton (1995).

25   For the background to the development of corporate governance since the 1970s, *see* Parkinson (2000, pp. 250–7).

26   Christopher Napier, 'The Unaccountable Robert Maxwell', *Accountancy*, vol. 109, issue 1182, February 1992, pp. 25–6.

27   Cadbury (1990).

28   *See* Appendix 2.1.

29   The Association of British Insurers and the National Association of Pension Funds had recommended that the role of chair and CEO be split before the first meeting of the Cadbury Committee. *See* David Owen and Richard Lapper, 'Life at the top gets riskier: Fallout since the 1987 crash', *Financial Times*, 15 November 1990, p. 27, and Colin Narbrough, 'NAPF seeks radical

changes; National Association of Pension Funds', *The Times*, 28 February, 1991.

30   The Minister for Corporate Affairs was concerned about the role of non-executive directors. *See* Richard Waters, 'Minister backs calls to reform board structure', *Financial Times*, 8 December 1990, p. 4.

31   *See* Norma Cohen, 'The Cadbury Report: Code of practice relies on threat of public censure', *Financial Times*, 28 May 1992, p. 12.

32   Cadbury Draft Report (1992, para. 3.6, p. 9).

33   Cadbury Draft Report (1992, para. 4.35, p. 20).

34   Cadbury Draft Report (1992, Appendix 2.4, pp. 56–7).

35   Cadbury Draft Report (1992, para. 1.3, p. 5).

36   Cadbury Draft Report (1992, paras 4.7–14, pp. 13–14).

37   *See* Lisa Buckingham, 'Business gives lukewarm approval to Cadbury plans', *The Guardian*, 13 August 1992.

38   For reports of these exchanges, *see* Clarke, T. (1993), 'Corporate Governance: The State of the Art', *Managerial Auditing Journal*, Vol. 8, No. 3, pp. 3–7, and Norma Cohen, 'CBI and IOD attack corporate governance reform plan', *Financial Times*, 30 July 1992, p. 18.

39   *See* Norma Cohen, 'Cadbury is backed by Exchange', *Financial Times*, 1 August 1992, p. 4, and Michael Cassell, 'Cadbury warns on boardroom best practice', *Financial Times*, 11 November 1992, p. 11.

40   *See* Norma Cohen, 'Cadbury plan for monitoring directors may be changed', *Financial Times*, 14 September 1992, p. 16.

41   *See* Lisa Buckingham, 'Of boards, buddies and bad practice: Many of Britain's blue chip companies would fail to meet proposed improvements in standards of corporate governance', *The Guardian*, 13 June 1992, p. 37, and Norma Cohen, 'Cadbury proposals prove unpalatable: Reaction to the report', *Financial Times*, 3 August 1992, p. 5.

42   For an early criticism of the Cadbury Report's weakness on internal audit, *see* Andrew Jack, 'Cadbury report criticised', *Financial Times*, 27 June 1992, p. 4.

43   *See* Andrew Jack, 'Doubts raised on Cadbury proposals', *Financial Times*, 7 August 1992, p. 6.

44   For an example of US influence, *see* Cadbury Report (1992, para. 4.33, p. 27) on audit committees. It was pointed out that in the US board sub-committees were more extensive but so were abuses of corporate power ('In Search of Better Boardrooms', *The Economist*, 30 May 1992, p. 13).

45   *See* Michael Cassell, 'Cadbury warns on boardroom best practice', *Financial Times*, 11 November 1992, p. 11.

46   *See* 'Call for directors to state reasons for resignation', *The Daily Telegraph*, 11 November 1992, p. 31.

47   *See* 'CBI loses out over Cadbury Report', *The Evening Standard Europe Intelligence Wire*, 24 November 1992.

48   *See* Lisa Buckingham, 'Cadbury drive to rebuild trust in the way business is run relies on market: Final code aims to stop buccaneers becoming pirates and lift earnings – Lack of enforcement agency flawed', *The Guardian*, 2 December 1992, p. 12.

49   Cadbury Report (1992, para. 1.8, p. 12).

50   *See* Richard Waters, Michael Cassell and Andrew Jack, 'Reservations underlie welcome for Cadbury', *Financial Times*, 2 December 1992, p. 12.

51 *See* 'City Comment: Cadbury's confection of woolly thinking', *The Daily Telegraph*, 2 December 1992.

52 *See* Andrew Jack, 'Report sets out an ambitious remit for self-regulation', *Financial Times*, 2 December 1992, p. 12.

53 *See* Lisa Buckingham, *The Guardian*, 2 December 1992, p. 12, *op. cit.*

54 *See* 'Benevolent dictatorships rule, OK', *Director*, August 1993, vol. 47, issue 1, p. 13; *see also* the negative comments of the CEO of Allied Textile Cos in 'Dealing with reality: A lesson for the City', *Accountancy*, March 1993, vol. 111, issue 1195, pp. 22–3. For a critique of the elevation of the role of the non-executive director, *see* 'A blatant slur on executive directors' integrity', *Accountancy*, April 1993, vol. 111, issue 1196, pp. 81–2. For other criticisms that the report had not gone far enough, *see* 'Good Corporate Governance needs a helping hand', *Accountancy*, January 1993, vol. 111, issue 1193, pp. 58–9.

55 *See* Cadbury Report (1992, paras 4.10–17, pp. 22–4) *and* Owen Green, 'Personal View: Why Cadbury leaves a bitter taste', *Financial Times*, 9 June 1992, p. 19.

56 This was a particular worry for the smaller companies; *see* 'An Unfairly Costly Code', *Management Today*, August 1993, p. 61 and Andrew Jack, 'Cadbury may add to audit fees', *Financial Times*, 3 December 1992, p. 9.

57 *See* 'Soft-centred/Cadbury on corporate governance', *The Economist*, 5 December 1992.

58 *See* Lisa Buckingham, *The Guardian*, 2 December 1992, p. 12, *op. cit.*

59 For a report on a survey of executives showing support for statutory backing for some of the reforms, *see* 'Statutory support for the Cadbury code?', *Management Accounting*, July/August 1992, vol. 71, issue 7, p. 4.

60 *See* J.A. Mitchell (1993), 'Poisoned Chocolate? Corporate Governance and the Cadbury Report', *Managerial Auditing Journal*, vol. 8, no. 3, pp. 31–4.

61 *See* Lisa Buckingham, 'Coded message many have decided to ignore: Survey finds only eight of the top 100 companies meet key criterion for boardroom scrutiny of appointments', *The Guardian*, 1 December 1992, p. 14.

62 *See* George Sivell, 'Big firms beat Cadbury deadline', *The Times*, 1 July 1993. Cadbury was active in his encouragement for them to do so (*see*, for example, 'Cadbury warns of regulatory threat', *Management Accounting*, June 1993, vol. 71, issue 6, p. 3).

63 *See* Lucy Kellaway, 'Companies act to split top roles, report shows', *Financial Times*, 14 July 1993, p. 7.

64 Rutteman Working Group (1994).

65 Committee on the Financial Aspects of Corporate Governance (1995).

66 A special committee was subsequently formed to look into this.

67 *See* Andrew Piper and Rowan Jones, 'Auditors' reviews of Cadbury compliance statements', *Management Accounting*, March 1995, vol. 73, issue 3, p. 29; and Rupert Morris, 'Cracking the Cadbury Code', *Management Today*, April 1995, p. 48.

68 For example, Norma Cohen, 'The Cadbury Report: Investors raise only two cheers', *Financial Times*, 28 May 1992, p. 12; 'City Comment: The fat pay packets of corporate governance', *The Daily Telegraph*, 30 March 1993; and Christopher Lorenz, 'Management: Time for Cadbury to tackle high pay', *Financial Times*, 4 June 1993, p. 14.

69 Cadbury Report (1992, para. 3.12, p. 18).
70 For a discussion of the history of the bank's role in the corporate governance debate, *see* 'The Bank and Corporate Governance: Past, present and future', *Bank of England Quarterly Bulletin*, August 1993, vol. 33, no. 3, pp. 388–92.
71 The Accounting Standards Board had been attempting to move towards full disclosure of executive pay but these moves had stalled (see Philip Ryland, 'A piece of Cadbury melts', *Investors Chronicle*, 22 April 1994, vol. 108, issue 1370, p. 6).
72 Cadbury Report (1992, para. 4.42, p. 31).
73 *See* Lisa Buckingham, 'Cadbury seeks curb on golden handshake deals', *The Guardian*, 18 February 1994, p. 19; and Nick Goodway, 'Business: Bosses give the cold shoulder to Cadbury – Hefty pay rises, lucrative perks and three-years contracts are still rife', *The Observer*, 23 October 1994, p. 5.
74 *See* Vanessa Houlder, Andrew Hill and Andrew Jack, 'Why do you deserve to be paid so much? A look at moves to counter criticism of big bonuses by establishing a better link with performance', *Financial Times*, 21 November 1994, p. 12; and Peter Rodgers, 'Pension funds want full disclosure of board-room pay', *The Independent*, 10 December 1994, Business p. 16. For aca-demic evidence on the weak link between executive pay and executive performance, *see* Conyon and Leech (1994).
75 *See* Michael White, Simon Beavis and Chris Barrie, 'CBI help sought over pay excesses: Ministers split over boardroom pay', *The Guardian*, 24 December 1994, p. 1; and William Lewis, 'The year of the tweaked snouts – the changing attitudes towards boardroom pay', *Financial Times*, 24 December 1994, p. 8.
76 *See* William Lewis, *Financial Times*, 24 December 1994, p. 8, *op. cit.*
77 For example, Conyon and Leech (1994).
78 *See* Roger Trapp, 'Rolling back the shadows: Roger Trapp looks at the trend to greater openness on executive perks', *The Independent*, 4 January, 1995, p. 26.
79 *See* William Lewis, 'Shareholders flex a muscle on top pay: A look at the options as Whitehall ponders ways of restraining directors' pay', *Financial Times*, 7 December 1994, p. 10.
80 *See* Michael White, Simon Beavis and Chris Barrie, *The Guardian*, 24 December 1994, p. 1, *op. cit.*
81 *See* Appendix 2.2.
82 Greenbury Report (1995, para. 8.1–12, pp. 49–52); and William Lewis, George Parker and Geoff Dyer, 'Greenbury urges shake-up of top pay structure at utilities', *Financial Times*, 12 July 1995, p. 20.
83 *See* Peter Rodgers, 'Pension funds hit out at Greenbury code on top pay', *The Independent*, 23 December 1996, Business p. 16.
84 Greenbury Report (1995, para. 4, pp. 21–5).
85 Greenbury Report (1995, para. 4.4, pp. 21–2).
86 *See* Lisa Buckingham, Simon Beavis and Michael White, 'Greenbury Report: 'Timid' enquiry fails to satisfy Labour – Opposition and unions accuse CBI committee of failing to find remedy for abuses in privatised utilities', *The Guardian*, 18 July 1995, p. 15.
87 *See* Lisa Buckingham, Simon Beavis and Michael White, 'Greenbury report provokes row on corporate greed', *The Guardian*, 18 July 1995, p. 1.
88 *See* Neil Collins, 'How jolly Greenbury giants have hurt the little people', *The Daily Telegraph*, 18 July 1995.

89 *See* Philip Bassett, 'Greenbury and Nolan failed, says IoD chief', *The Times*, 1 November 1995; and Michael Cassell, 'CBI chief fears policy 'reversion' by Labour', *Financial Times*, 9 November 1995, p. 13.

90 *See* William Lewis, 'Business leaders want end to boardroom reform', *Financial Times*, 25 October, 1995, p. 10.

91 'Leading Article: Backlash after Greenbury', *Financial Times*, 13 November 1995, p. 21.

92 *See* Peter Rodgers, 'Economic View: The Greenbury effect – is it pushing pay higher? Greater circulation of information is responsible for accelerating pay rises', *The Independent*, 26 April 1996, Business p. 21. *See also* Conyon, Clarke and Peck (1998).

93 That is not to say that a radically different governance system would not reduce executive pay. Executive pay is much lower as a multiple of average earnings in Japan than it is the UK, while UK executive pay is in turn a much lower multiple of earnings than it is in US.

94 *See* DTI (1999), *Secretary of State's Speech, 19 July 1999: Directors' Remuneration*.

95 *See* DTI *Press Release*, P/2001/132, 'Byers to strengthen link between boardroom pay and performance', 7 March 2001.

96 *See* DTI *Press Release*, P/2001/572, 'Shareholders to get annual vote on directors' pay', 23 October 2001.

97 Customers and unions were involved in the public protests outside the British Gas AGM in 1995. *See* Eric Reguly, 'Gas investors call in Cedric the pig but lose out to the City', *The Times*, 1 June 1995.

98 Greenbury complained of 'media harassment and personal intrusion'; *see* William Lewis, 'Remit row delays Cadbury successor', *Financial Times*, 9 November 1995, p. 11.

99 Cadbury Report (1992, para. 3.12, p. 18)

100 *See* Norma Cohen, 'Management: A taste for Cadbury', Financial Times, 14 June 1995, p. 19; for a recognition by Adrian Cadbury of the crucial role of Stock Exchange support for his proposals, *see* Norma Cohen, 'Cadbury claims high rate of compliance with code', *Financial Times*, 25 May 1995, p. 12.

101 *See* Roger Cowe, 'Weinstock bows out with attack on "erosion of trust"', *The Guardian*, 7 September 1996, p. 26 on Lord Weinstock's retirement speech from GEC.

102 *See* Norma Cohen, 'Lipworth sets out agenda for Cadbury 2: Move to cut corporate code's emphasis on role of non-executive directors', *Financial Times*, 29 April 1995, p. 4.

103 *See* William Lewis, *Financial Times*, 9 November 1995, p. 11, *op. cit.*

104 *See* Norma Cohen and William Lewis, 'Cadbury successor may change board reforms: ICI chairman to head new corporate watchdog', *Financial Times*, 23 November 1995, p. 24.

105 Hampel Report (1998, para. 2, p. 5).

106 For the members of the committee, *see* Appendix 2.3.

107 *See* Christy Chapman, '"Cadbury II" begins work', *The Internal Auditor*, April 1996, vol. 53, issue 2, p. 9.

108 *See* William Lewis and David Wighton, 'Management: Labour softens on stakeholding: The opposition has opted for cultural change', *Financial Times*, 26 June 1996, p. 19.

109 *See* William Lewis and David Wighton, *Financial Times*, 26 June 1996, p. 19, *op. cit.*

110 *See* Lindsay Percival-Straunik, 'The Hampel Committee: Opportunity Knocked', *Director*, October 1997, vol. 51, issue 3, pp. 46–51.

111 *See* 'Comment: Sir Ronald looks for reform not revolution', *The Independent*, 9 December 1995, Business p. 24.

112 'Respondents to Hampel Favour Freedom', *Accountancy*, February 1997, vol. 119, issue 1242, p. 10.

113 *See* Jason Nisse, 'Hampel Committee extends deadline', *The Times*, 3 January 1997.

114 *See* Roger Cowe, 'Finance: Board reform hopes dashed: The Hampel Report', *The Guardian*, 6 August 1997, p. 18.

115 *See* Neil Cowan, 'Hampel falls short', *The Internal Auditor*, December 1997, vol. 54, issue 6, p. 96; Lindsay Percival-Straunik, 'The Hampel Report: clear enough?', *Director*, September 1997, vol. 51, issue 2, p. 22, suggests that not enough may have been done to avert legal intervention. Tricker (1998) is very critical of the non-inclusive nature of the discussions that surrounded the Hampel Report.

116 *See* William Lewis, 'Hampel "omissions" attacked: Institutions criticise "hole at heart" of corporate governance report', *Financial Times*, 11 August 1997, p. 1.

117 'City: IoD seeks guide for incentives', *The Daily Telegraph*, 22 September 1997.

118 'Beefed-up Hampel on the cards', *People Management*, 20 November 1997, vol. 3, issue 23, p. 19 and Celia Weston, 'CBI conference: Beckett hints at beefing up corporate governance', *The Guardian*, 12 November 1997, p. 23.

119 *See* Antony Barnett, 'Business: Hampel report snubs pleas for tougher rules', *The Observer*, 21 December 1997, p. 1.

120 *See* Jane Martinson, 'Hampel set to create corporate "supercode"', *Financial Times*, 22 October 1997, p. 12.

121 Hampel Report (1998, para. 4.12, p. 36).

122 *See* Alasdair Murray, 'Hampel report prompts Beckett review', *The Times*, 29 January 1998.

123 *See* Jane Martinson, 'The Hampel Report: Plea to give self-regulation "time to work"', *Financial Times*, 29 January 1998, p. 11.

124 *See* Nigel Cope, 'Business: Supercode is 'weak, bland and useless', *The Independent*, 25 June 1998, Business p. 19. Parkinson and Kelly (1999) suggest that the flaw in the UK approach to corporate governance is that it relies on shareholder pressure for enforcement and that this is very weak. The Hampel Report continued the tradition of relying on this mechanism.

125 *See* Stock *et al.* (1999).

126 *See* Nick Goodway, 'Survey shows UK governance still leads world', *London Financial News*, 29 June 1998.

127 *See* Jim Kelly, 'Supercode would have made Maxwell a saint: Corporate Governance magazine makes 1991 comparison', *Financial Times*, 2 May 1998, p. 8.

128 *See* David Band and Allan Blake, 'Adaptability is the secret of success: To survive in the long term, companies must learn from the wider implications of the Hampel report', *The Independent*, 22 April 1998.

129 Turnbull Report (1999, para. 20, p. 7).

130   Hampel Report (1998, para. 6.14, p. 54).
131   *See* Jim Kelly, 'Listed groups face tougher rules on managing risks: Turnbull requirements tightened up since draft stage', *Financial Times*, 27 September 1999, p. 28. For membership of the committee, *see* Appendix 2.4.
132   Turnbull Report (1999, p. 1).
133   *See* Jim Kelly, 'Corporate "supercode" will urge tighter control of internal risks', *Financial Times*, 19 April 1999, p. 22.
134   *See* Susannah Kingsmill, 'Turnbull and transparency: companies are being forced into a radical reassessment of their internal controls', *London Financial News*, 4 October 1999.
135   *See* Roger Cowe, 'Risk Evaluation: Making Maxwells a thing of the past: The Turnbull report on companies' internal controls will oblige them to address issues from health to the environment', *The Guardian*, 23 October 1999, p. 30.
136   *See* Turnbull Report (1999, p. 15).
137   *See* speech by Margaret Beckett on whether the Government can encourage the private sector in the area of corporate governance (Margaret Beckett, *Speech at PIRC Annual Conference*, March 1998, *www.dti.gov.uk/Minspeech/pircfin.htm*).
138   DTI (1998, para. 3.2).
139   DTI (1998, para. 3.7).
140   DTI (1998, para. 3.7).
141   DTI (1998, para. 5.2).
142   *See* Appendix 2.5.
143   DTI (1999, 2000a, 2000b and 2001) available from *www.dti.gov.uk/cld/*
144   DTI (2001, p. xvii) and Brian Singleton-Green, 'UK: Law Company Law Review – Reform List', *Accountancy*, 30 September 2001.
145   Wilson (2000) notes the change in direction in the DTI initiated by Beckett's successor, Peter Mandelson. His successor, Stephen Byers, suggested a change in focus from corporates to an encouragement of the engagement of shareholders in activism (Stephen Byers, *Speech at PIRC Annual Conference*, March, 1999, *www.dti.gov.uk/Minspeech/byers250399.htm*). He also suggested that he was still monitoring the performance of the corporate governance system (Stephen Byers, *Directors' Remuneration*, July 1999, *www.dti.gov.uk/Minspeech/byers190799.htm*). However, in 2000 Byers moved the emphasis away from stakeholding, suggesting the most of corporate governance would be delegated to the Financial Reporting Council (Stephen Byers, *Speech at TUC/IPPR Seminar on Corporate Governance*, June 2000, *www.dti.gov.uk/Minspeech/byers070600.htm*).
146   *See* Christine Buckley, 'Monks calls company law review "a cop out"', *The Times*, 23 August 2000, p. 22.
147   *See* Ian McConnell, 'CBI opposes laws requiring firms to reveal public interest details', *The Herald*, 7 August 2000, p. 18.
148   *See* Christine Buckley, 'UK: Reforms could start quiet revolution', *The Times*, 27 July 2001, p. 26 and Kevin Brown and Michael Peel, 'Blueprint to help bring business "into 21st century"', *Financial Times*, 27 July 2001.
149   DTI (1996). A second Myners Report appeared in 2001 (HM Treasury, 2001).
150   Cadbury (2000).

151 The bank sold Pro-NED in early 1994. *See* Norma Cohen, 'Pro-NED sold off to European headhunting company', *Financial Times*, 19 January 1994, p. 20.
152 *See* Whittington (1993).
153 *See* Rupert Morris, *Management Today*, April 1995, pp. 48, *op. cit.*

References

Boyd, C. (1996) 'Ethics and Corporate Governance: The Issues Raised by the Cadbury Report in the United Kingdom', *Journal of Business Ethics*, vol. 15, no. 2, pp. 167–208.

Cadbury, A. (1990) *The Company Director*, London: Director Books.

Cadbury, A. (2000) 'The Corporate Governance Agenda', *Corporate Governance*, vol. 8, no. 1, pp. 7–15.

Charkham, J.P. (1994) *Keeping Good Company: a study of corporate governance in five countries*, Oxford: Oxford University Press.

Committee on Corporate Governance (1998) *Final Report* [Hampel Report], London: Gee Publishing.

Committee on the Financial Aspects of Corporate Governance (1992) *Report with Code of Best Practice* [Cadbury Report], London: Gee Publishing.

Committee on the Financial Aspects of Corporate Governance (1992) *Draft Report* [Cadbury Draft Report], London: Gee Publishing.

Committee on the Financial Aspects of Corporate Governance (1995) *Compliance with the Code of Best Practice*, London: Gee Publishing.

Conyon, M., Clarke, R. and Peck, S. (1998) 'Corporate governance and directors' remuneration: views from the top', *Business Strategy Review*, vol. 9, no. 4, pp. 21–30.

Conyon, M. and Leech, D.J. (1994) 'Top Pay, Company Performance and Corporate Governance', *Oxford Bulletin of Economics and Statistics*, vol. 56, no. 3, pp. 229–47.

Cook, J. and Deakin, S. (1999) 'Chapter 10: Empirical Evidence on Corporate Control', in ESRC Centre for Business Research, *Literature Survey on Factual, Empirical and Legal Issues*, Cambridge: ESRC Centre for Business Research at *www.dti.gov.uk/cld/esrc10pdf*

DTI (1996) *Developing a Winning Partnership* [Myners Report], London: DTI.

DTI (1998) *Modern Company Law for a Competitive Economy*, London: DTI at *www.dti.gov.uk/cld/reviews/condocs.htm*

DTI (1999) *Modern Company Law for a Competitive Economy: The Strategic Framework*, London: DTI at *www.dti.gov.uk/cld/reviews/condocs.htm*

DTI (2000a) *Modern Company Law for a Competitive Economy: Developing the Framework*, London: DTI at *www.dti.gov.uk/cld/reviews/condocs.htm*

DTI (2000b) *Modern Company Law for a Competitive Economy: Completing the Structure*, London: DTI at *www.dti.gov.uk/cld/reviews/condocs.htm*

DTI (2001) *Modern Company Law for a Competitive Economy: Final Report*, London: DTI at *www.dti.gov.uk/cld/final_report/index.htm*

Finch, V. (1992) 'Board Performance and Cadbury on Corporate Governance', *Journal of Business Law*, pp. 581–95.

Franks, J. and Mayer, C. (1990) 'Capital Markets and Corporate Control: A Study of France, Germany and the UK', *Economic Policy*, April, pp. 189–231.

HM Treasury (2001) *Institutional Investment in the United Kingdom: A Review* [Myners Report, 2001], London: HM Treasury.

Hutton, W. (1995) *The State We're In*, London: Vintage.

ICEAW (1999) *Internal Control – Guidance for Directors on the Combined Code* [Turnbull Report], London: Institute of Chartered Accountants in England and Wales.

Jones, I.W. and Pollitt, M.G. (1996) 'Economics, Ethics and Integrity in Business' *Journal of General Management*, vol. 21, no. 3, pp. 30–47.

Jones, I.W. and Pollitt, M.G. (eds) (1998) *The Role of Business Ethics in Economic Performance*, Basingstoke: Palgrave Macmillan/St Martin's Press.

Kay, J. and Silbertson, A. (1995) 'Corporate governance', *National Institute Economic Review*, vol. 153, pp. 84–99.

Monks, R.A.G., (2000) 'Modern Company Law for a Competitive Economy: the strategic framework', *Corporate Governance*, vol. 8, no. 1, pp. 16–24.

OECD (1991) *OECD Economic Outlook July 1991*, Paris: OECD.

Parkinson, J. (2000) 'Evolution and Policy in Company Law: The Non-Executive Director', in J. Parkinson, A. Gamble and G. Kelly (eds), *The Political Economy of the Company*, Oxford: Hart Publishing.

Parkinson, J. (2002) 'Inclusive Company Law', in J. de Lacy (ed.), *The Reform of Company Law in the UK*, London: Cavendish.

Parkinson, J. and Kelly, G. (1999) 'The Combined Code on Corporate Governance', *Political Quarterly*, vol. 70, pp. 101–7.

Rutteman Working Group (1994) *Internal Control and Financial Reporting: Guidance for directors of listed companies registered in the UK* [Rutteman Report], London: Rutteman Working Group.

Study Group on Directors' Remuneration (1995) *Directors' Remuneration: Report of a Study Group Chaired by Sir Richard Greenbury* [Greenbury Report], London: Gee Publishing.

Stock, M., Copnell, T. and Wicks, C. (1999) *The Combined Code – A Practical Guide*, London: Gee Publishing.

Tricker, B. (1998) 'Editorial: Platitudes parading as paradigms', *Corporate Governance*, vol. 6, no. 1, pp. 2–4.

Turnbull, S. (1997) 'Corporate Governance: its Scope, Concerns and Theories', *Corporate Governance*, vol. 5, no. 4, pp. 180–205.

Whittington, G. (1993) 'Corporate Governance and the Regulation of Financial Reporting', *Accounting and Business Research*, vol. 23, no. 91, p. 311.

Wilson, G. (2000) 'Business, State and Community: Responsible Risk Takers. New Labour and the Governance of Corporate Business', *Journal of Law and Society*, vol. 27, no. 1, pp. 151–77.

Appendixes

Appendix 2.1: Members of the Cadbury Committee

Name	Occupation
Sir Adrian Cadbury	
Ian Butler	Council member, CBI and former Chairman, CBI Companies Committee
Jim Butler	Senior partner, KPMG Peat Marwick

Jonathan Charkham	Advisor to the Governor of Bank of England
Hugh Collum	Chairman, Hundred Group of Finance Directors
Sir Ron Dearing	Chairman, Financial Reporting Council
Andrew Likierman	Professor of Accounting and Financial Control London Business School
Nigel Macdonald	Vice President, Institute of Chartered Accountants of Scotland
Mike Sandland	Chairman, Institutional Shareholders Committee
Mark Sheldon	President, Law Society
Sir Andrew Hugh Smith	Chairman, London Stock Exchange
Sir Dermot de Trafford, Bt	Chairman, Institute of Directors
Observers	
Mrs Sarah Brown (until October 1991)	Head of Companies Division, DTI
Mr Arthur Russell (from November 1991)	Head of Companies Division, DTI
Secretary	
Nigel Peace	Secondment from DTI
Advisor	
Sir Christopher Hogg	Chairman, Reuters Holdings PLC

Source: Cadbury Report (1992, pp. 61–2).

Appendix 2.2: Members of the Greenbury Committee

Name	Occupation
Sir Richard Greenbury	Chairman, Marks and Spencer Plc
Sir Michael Angus	Chairman, Whitbread Plc and the Boots Company Plc
Sir David Chapman, Bt	Wise Speke Limited (stockbrokers), Newcastle
Sir Denys Henderson	Chairman, Rank Organisation Plc
Sir David Lees	Chairman, GKN Plc
Mr Geoff Lindey	Head of UK Institutional Investment JP Morgan Investment Management Inc
Mr Tim Melville Ross	Director, General Institute of Directors
Mr George Metcalfe	Chairman and CEO, UMECO Plc
Sir David Simon	Chairman, The British Petroleum Company Plc
Sir Ian Vallance	Chairman, British Telecommunications Plc
Sir Robert Walther	Group Chief Executive, Clerical Medical Investment Group

Appendix 2.2 (*Continued*)

Name	Occupation
Professional advisors	
Mr Andrew Edwards	
Mr John Grieves	Freshfields
Mr Peter Jeffcote	Freshfields
Mr Angus Maitland	Maitland Consultancy
Mr John Carney	Towers Perrin
Secretary	
Mr Matt Lewis	KPMG, Secretary to the Group

Source: Greenbury Report (1995, p. 5).

Appendix 2.3: Members of the Hampel Committee

Name	Occupation
Sir Ronald Hampel	Chairman, ICI
Michael Coppel	Chairman, Airsprung Furniture Group
Michael Hartnall	Finance Director, Rexam Plc
Giles Henderson, CBE	Senior Partner, Slaughter and May
Sir Nigel Mobbs	Executive Chairman, Slough Estates Plc
Tony Richards, TD	Director, Henderson Costhwaite Ltd
Tom Ross	Principal and Actuary, Aon Consulting Limited
Peter Smith	Chairman, Coopers and Lybrand
David Thomas	Director and General Manager (Investments), Equitable Life Assurance Society
Sir Clive Thompson	Chief Executive, Rentokil Initial Plc
Lord Simon	Chairman, BP Plc (resigned 7 May 1997)
Christopher Haskins	Chairman, Northern Foods Plc (resigned August 1997)
Secretary	
John Healey	

Source: Hampel Report (1998, p. 65).

Appendix 2.4: Members of the Turnbull Committee

Name	Occupation
Nigel Turnbull (Chairman)	Executive Director, Rank Group Plc
Roger Davis (Deputy Chairman)	Head of Professional Affairs, PriceWaterhouseCoopers

Douglas Flint	Group Finance Director, HSBC Holdings Plc
Huw Jones	Director of Corporate Finance, Prudential Portfolio Managers
David Lindsell	Partner, Ernst and Young
Tim Rowbury	Internal Audit Consultant
Jonathan Southern	Director of Accounting and Reporting, Diageo Plc
David Wilson	Company Secretary and General Counsel, Debenhams Plc
Staff	
Anthony Carey	Project Director, Institute of Chartered Accountants in England and Wales (ICAEW)
Jonathan Hunt	Project Manager, ICAEW

Source: Turnbull Report (1999, p. 15).

Appendix 2.5: Members of Company Law Review Steering Group

Name	Occupation
Richard Rogers (Chairman)	Director, Company Law and Investigations, Department of Trade and Industry
The Right Hon. Lady Justice Mary Arden, DBE	
Robert Bertram	Formerly Partner, Shepherd and Wedderburn WS
Sir Bryan Carsberg	Former Secretary-General, International Accounting Standards Committee
Paul Davies	Cassel Professor of Commercial Law, London School of Economics and Political Science
Sir Stuart Hampson	Chairman, John Lewis Partnership plc
John Kay	Director, London Economics [until March 2000]
John Parkinson	Professor of Law, University of Bristol
Colin Perry	Chairman, LTE Scientific Ltd
John Plender	Broadcaster and journalist
Rosemary Radcliffe, CBE	Chief Economist, PriceWaterhouse-Coopers
Jonathan Rickford, CBE	Company Law Review Project Director

Appendix 2.5 (*Continued*)

Name	Occupation
Bryan Sanderson, CBE	Chairman, Learning and Skills Council; Chairman, BUPA; Former Group Managing Director, BP Amoco Plc
Martin Scicluna	Chairman, Deloitte & Touche
Richard Sykes, QC	Chairman, Financial Reporting Review Panel

Source: *http://www.dti.gov.uk/cld/members.htm*

Comments by Robert M. Worcester

Nothing happens unless people make it happen. The composition and commissioning of the committees that have driven the debate on corporate governance is extremely important – though Jones and Pollitt mentioned this factor, the chapter does not develop it in any great detail. In particular, of course, the chairman of such a committee is highly influential; but they didn't interview the chairman in any of the cases they studied, only another member of the committee. I think that if the chairmen had had the opportunity to comment on the chapter, a subtly different picture would have emerged.

The corporate governance debate has not arisen in isolation. Parallel trends have been evident in the civic sector and in the public sector as well as corporations. For example, at the International Social Science Council, based at UNESCO, a decade ago, a constitutional committee was set up under my chairmanship to bring its 1946 constitution into the 1990s, bringing in many of the principles of transparency, rotation, declaration of conflicts, and so on, to its operations; a similar committee was established at WWF, World Wide Fund for Nature (formerly World Wildlife Fund) which also established some of the same principles. I know of other organisations in the civic and public sector that have done the same.

The question of where power lies within a company has been central to the corporate governance debate, and the recommendations have tended to be round on the dispersion and diffusion of that power, for example, by splitting the roles of chief executive and chairman. Our current model of corporate governance involves a separation of powers. That may be a useful protection against the abuse of power, but it can hamper the company in other ways. The evidence is that where the chairman and chief executive roles are combined, the companies are more effective. BTR and Lord Weinstock are a case in point; at GEC it was very clear who ran the company although there was artificial segmentation. By contrast, the British banks had a very high proportion of non-executives but the evidence was that they weren't very well governed in the first place.

There has been a substantial decline in public confidence in institutions in general: confidence was high in the 1960s but declined in the 1970s and has remained low ever since. The chapter indicates that Robert

Maxwell's practices triggered or crystallised the movement towards focus on governance; it was, in my view, on the move long before his activities were brought to the attention of the community. In 1976, MORI was commissioned by the CBI to examine many of these issues and how they played in the public's mind. The scandal at Lloyds of London occurred, after all, in 1991 when huge losses three years earlier were brought to bear on investors.

It is too much of a simplification to view the influence of the media as a single phenomenon: different media outlets have different degrees of influence. In particular, the role of the *Financial Times* is generally bigger than all the other newspapers. Reverting to Maxwell, it was the BBC *Panorama* programme that 'blew the whistle' on Maxwell's *Mirror* 'Spot the Ball' competition, which so rigged the game that no one could win. It is true that the popular press got in the act on Cedric Brown, then CEO of British Gas, but he was the lightning rod which became blown out of all proportion. Reaction to the Greenbury Report was very negative – but they would have torn him apart even if he had brought the ten commandments, as Sir Richard's lustre had by then been tarnished by the fading performance of Marks & Spencer, of which he was Chairman and generally acknowledged to be in charge.

Public interest in some of the issues with which corporate governance is associated should not be confused with interest in corporate governance itself. In the Cedric Brown case, for example, it would not have diverted resentment at his pay rise if his salary had been determined in a different way. The details of corporate governance are never likely to interest the public. Public opinion is not interested in process. What the public want to know is if they are getting a fair shake of the stick and whether someone decent and honourable is looking after their interests. What will determine the reputation of British business with the public will not be whether companies follow the recommendations of the various committees, but whether there are or are not further scandals.

3

Agricultural Biotechnology Hanging in the Balance: Why the Anti-GM Food Campaign has been so Successful

Sue Mayer

Introduction

In 1996, genetically modified (GM) soybean was grown commercially in the USA for the first time. The soybeans had been made tolerant to a herbicide, glyphosate (Roundup) made by Monsanto. By growing the GM soybeans, farmers could spray the broad-spectrum herbicide on the crop without it being damaged and, thereby, weed control was made easier. Soybeans are a commodity crop and traded globally, so the GM soybeans were mixed with conventional ones and shipped across the world. As the soybeans were first imported into Europe at the end of 1996, Greenpeace revealed the movement of the GM soybeans and that they, or their derivatives (such as soybean oil or lecithin), would be found in around 60 per cent of processed foods on supermarket shelves and would not be labelled.[1]

Thus began the backlash against GM foods. Monsanto and the other biotechnology companies denied that GM soybean could be segregated (the cost savings of bulk markets would be lost) or that labels based on the means of production were justified. They argued that there was no reason in safety terms why they should be discriminated against and that to do so would contravene trade rules. The public in the UK and the rest of Europe disagreed that choice should be denied and campaigns started to get GM ingredients removed from foods. But Europe has been at the centre of the rejection of GM foods, resistance has spread to many other parts of the world, including developing countries.

As a result of the campaigns, it is almost impossible to buy food in the UK which contains GM ingredients. The 'life sciences' model of industry, with the fusion of agricultural and human biotechnology, has been disrupted. Mergers and acquisitions were the focus of the mid-1990s and into 1998, but then stopped abruptly. In 2000 and 2001, companies such as Novartis, AstraZeneca and Aventis, have sold off their agrochemical divisions. Although field trials continue, no GM crops are grown commercially in Europe and prospects over the next decade look bleak.

This chapter considers the history of this collapse of the agricultural-biotechnology industry in Europe and the lessons to be learned from it. Most importantly, it argues that the success of the campaigns run by NGOs cannot be attributed to scaremongering opportunism or media-inspired hysteria. NGOs run many campaigns, few of which connect with the public in the way in which the GM-foods issue has. A whole spectrum of concerns is embodied in the GM-food debate, including:

- the ability of science to predict harm
- whether institutions will act impartially in uncertain situations
- the extent to which markets will allow choice
- how international trade rules affect consumers and
- the effective exclusion of ethical matters from decisions.

All of these concerns are soundly and rationally based. Industry, regulators and politicians have to recognise their legitimacy and engage with them if agricultural biotechnology is to find a sustainable future.

Public opinion and the history of GM food collapse

To appreciate the roots of the current crisis, it is necessary to examine policy decisions in the late 1980s and early 1990s, when GM crops began being tested. In Europe, as in the USA, the new genetic technologies were seen as drivers of an industrial renaissance and as being fundamental to competitiveness. Thus, the regulatory approach was intended to encourage the development of the biotechnology industry while safeguarding the environment and human health.[2] It contained the in-built policy assumption that biotechnology and GMOs represented a positive future for agriculture in Europe (Levidow, 1994).

In these early stages of the technology's development, as financial and intellectual commitments were made to specific trajectories, there was little meaningful public debate. Several NGOs, including Greenpeace International and Friends of the Earth Europe, were articulating concerns but because there were no obvious public campaigns, tended to be dismissed. Critical questioning was equated with a lack of knowledge about the technology.

Equating questioning with ignorance was a fundamental mistake on behalf of the industry and regulators; it was not supported by the information available at the time from public-attitude research. For example, comparing the results of Eurobarometer surveys in 1991, 1993 and 1996 shows that while basic knowledge about the technology has increased, optimism about its ability to improve the quality of life has decreased.[3]

In addition, in what should have been a wake-up call, the 1996 Eurobarometer results confirmed other research showing that on GM foods, environmental and consumer groups were much more trusted sources of information than public bodies or companies. Eurobarometer also demonstrated that 74 per cent of the European public supported the labelling of GM foods; 60 per cent believed there should be public consultation about new developments; and just over half, 53 per cent, felt current regulations insufficient to protect people from the risks of the technology.

However, relying on opinion poll information alone does not provide a good basis for measuring public attitudes, as it reveals little about underlying concerns and can be heavily biased by the way in which a question is asked. Qualitative research is much more useful in understanding what shapes opinion and has shown that, for example, the British public have considerably mixed feelings about GM foods and the adequacy of present systems of regulations and of official 'scientific' assurances of safety, especially given the knowledge gained during the BSE crisis (Grove-White *et al.*, 1997).

This and similar research from the Netherlands (Hamstra, 1995) also showed that the public are discriminating in how they judge GM technologies, looking more favourably on applications, especially in the medical domain, where a clear social benefit is seen.

Applications which give benefits to, say, food processors are viewed less favourably since benefits appear restricted to certain financial interests. The public also displays awareness – and negative evaluation – of the interests driving GM innovations which are slanted to the affluent markets of the developed world rather than the needs of poor countries. The ultimate trajectory of the technology also plays in the public mind, with the concern that apparently innocuous uses may lead to misapplication in the future which they may be unable to control.

Thus, the public appears to bring together issues of trust, control, the controlling purposes and the particular costs and benefits of the application when evaluating the effects of GM technology. Public expressions of concern also show ethical judgements to be part of risk judgements.

The public are, therefore, making rather complex and sophisticated judgements in forming their attitudes towards GMOs.

The blanket approval (for reasons of competitiveness) of GM crops coming from European institutions and industry was, therefore, at odds with the more differentiated and considered approach of the public. The belief that, at the very least, the market should allow choice on such a sensitive subject was firmly embedded before the first GM foods were imported in 1996–97. The rejection of labelling and the legitimacy for it set industry and regulators in direct conflict with public opinion.

However, it was not to be either the biotechnology industry or governments which responded first to consumer concerns. It was the food producers and retailers, in direct contact with consumers, who realised that GM foods were not going to sell.

During 1999, there was a dramatic move out of the use of GM ingredients by food retailers and food processing companies in the UK. The Iceland supermarket chain had thrown down the gauntlet in March 1998 by going GM-free but others resisted until consumer pressure became too great. In March 1999, there was a positive scramble to change positions and by the turn of the century GM foods were off the UK menu.

The role of NGOs

The NGO campaign, spearheaded by environmental groups including Greenpeace, Friends of the Earth and the organic movement, around GM foods was very different from the way in which many campaigns had been run in the past. Rather than conventional political lobbying, the campaign was waged in the market place. The major supermarket chains and food producers, such as Unilever, Nestlé and Danone, were targets for these campaigns. Simple actions by many people (such as telephoning company care lines) was able to influence the food producers in ways that no amount of political work would.

However, it would not be true to claim that the public were simply scared into action by claims of the horrors of 'Frankenstein Foods'. The extraordinary spectrum of groups campaigning on GM foods (over 100 national organisations in the UK have joined the Five Year Freeze campaign for a moratorium on the commercial use of GM crops, animals and foods) includes aid agencies, women's groups, religious groups, trade unions, environmental and health organisations, and illustrates the depth and breadth of concerns GM foods touched.

There were several key parts of the campaign which together engaged the public and resonated with their broader concerns about risk and governance. These were that:

- the risks were real and different
- the regulations were not comprehensive
- people were being denied choice
- the products were not needed
- organic agriculture would be a victim
- Government was not impartial
- consumers could make a difference.

To see how the picture built up, it is worth considering each part in more detail.

The risks are real and different

There is considerable scientific evidence to draw upon to demonstrate that the use of GM crops and foods could bring risks to the environment and that the likelihood and impact of these is poorly understood. Emphasising the uncertainties and potential for surprises in terms of environmental and food safety was a key dimension of the debate. Illustrating that many independent scientists[4] and official bodies (such as the Royal Commission on Environmental Pollution (1989) and Government advisory committees)[5] had recognised that harm could arise was important. The risks highlighted were very broadly based and include those listed below.

1. Direct environmental effects:

- if there is gene transfer from the GM crop to native flora or fauna, which could lead to new pests as a result of hybridisation
- unexpected behaviour of the GM plant in the environment if it escapes its intended use and becomes a pest
- disruption of natural communities through competition or interference
- food web effects through harm to non-target species – for example, if the host range of a virus was increased, it may affect beneficial as well as the targeted species or there may be secondary effects of the insect toxin contained in a crop on the food web
- harmful effects on ecosystem processes if products of GM crops interfere with natural biochemical cycles

- squandering natural biological resources if, for example, the use of a genetic modification to bring pest resistance in many different species induces the emergence of resistance and loss of efficacy.

2. Indirect environmental effects:

- continuation of intensive agricultural systems as a result of the requirement for high levels of external inputs
- impacts on biodiversity as a consequence of changes in agricultural practice – for example, by altering patterns of herbicide use, effects on flora may be seen
- cumulative environmental impacts from multiple releases and interactions
- alterations in agricultural practices – for example, to manage any direct environment impacts such the evolution of insect, herbicide or disease resistance in weeds.

3. Health:

- new allergens being formed through the inclusion of novel proteins that trigger allergic reactions at some stage
- antibiotic resistance genes used as 'markers' in the GM food being transferred to gut micro-organisms and intensifying problems with antibiotic-resistant pathogens
- the creation of new toxins – for example through unexpected interactions between the product of the GM and other constituents.

The regulations are not comprehensive

An important dimension of the argument was that the systems for managing the risks of GM foods were not robust. In the case of releasing GM crops into the environment, the risk assessment process involves considering whether the gene(s) introduced into the GM crop could spread to related wild plants and what consequences this might have on an ecosystem. It also includes predicting whether the GM crop itself could become a troublesome weed. Risk management measures then include things such as separation distances between the GM crop and non-GM crops (to reduce the chance of pollen transfer), cleaning farming equipment between GM and non-GM crops to reduce spread, and the use of a herbicide to destroy any problem weeds that might emerge.

To investigate the risks, a step-by-step, case-by-case approach is taken. Experiments are conducted in the laboratory and then in the field, with gradually declining containment if it is deemed safe to do so. The presumption is that at each stage hazards will be accurately identified and that management techniques used will prevent any harm arising. While this process sounds straightforward and sensible, it is inevitably riddled with scientific uncertainty and subjective judgements. For example, what is included in the scope of harm is a matter of debate. Until 1998, the wider impacts of growing a GM crop on biodiversity if it alters agricultural practice (such as with herbicide-tolerant crops altering the pattern of herbicide use towards broader spectrum chemicals), was not considered in the risk assessment. It is only now being included as a result of external pressure from NGOs (Levidow and Carr, 2000a).

When potential adverse effects are included in an assessment, knowledge may be incomplete and contradictory. It is not only with complex indirect effects that knowledge is incomplete; even in what might be considered the more direct effect of gene flow, there are no simple answers. As more information is gathered about gene flow to wild, related plants, this is considered inevitable for some crops in Europe, such as oilseed rape and sugar beet (Lutman, 1999), although currently it is not possible to determine its frequency. The complexities of the environment mean that a host of factors, including geography and weather, will influence how far pollen moves. Thus, prediction becomes extremely difficult and the focus of the question has to turn to whether gene flow matters, and whether any adverse effects could be controlled by risk-management measures. These demand subjective judgements to be made about the acceptability of a risk and whether risk management is likely to be effective. For example, while sounding effective on paper, risk management plans may not be so easily followed in a farm situation. Separation distances between crops to reduce gene flow may not be observed and cleaning of equipment may not be plausible on busy farms with uncontrollable factors such as the weather.

Similarly, the process in place to determine the safety of consuming GM foods is also contestable. The approach to assessing the safety of GM ingredients is based on the principle of 'Substantial Equivalence' – if a food is substantially equivalent to the conventional counterpart, it is deemed to be safe. This approach evolved from international discussions, notably in the OECD, in the late 1980s and early 1990s and involves a comparison of various agronomic, biochemical, chemical and nutritional parameters of the GM food relative to existing conventionally produced foods. The composition of macro- and micro-nutrients, known toxins and other anti-nutritional factors are all measured. For example, in potato the macro-nutrients include carbohydrate and protein; the micro-nutrients are any vitamins or minerals and known toxins would include solanine (the compound which causes illness if poorly cooked green potatoes are eaten). However, there is no standard list of what components must be measured and, crucially, the approach relies on chemical composition being an accurate predictor of biological activity, an assumption which has been questioned (Millstone *et al.*, 1999). Furthermore, the system will struggle to identify unexpected changes or be able accurately to determine the allergic potential of the introduction of novel proteins into the diet from sources that have not been part of the human diet before. The Royal Society of Canada (2001) and the UK's Medical Research Council (2000) have recognised these issues – the difficulty of monitoring for health effects of consuming GM foods and the need for further research.

People are being denied choice

One of the areas which has generated considerable public anger is the lack of choice and it is an issue that has made the subject so difficult for food producers and retailers who rely on a rhetoric of choice.

At a time when public confidence in institutions is low, people feel increasingly that they have to rely on their own judgements about safety. People who have moral concerns about products on various grounds, such as animal welfare, want to be able to act according to their beliefs. In a market economy, one way judgements can be exercised and moral beliefs followed is in what a person buys. In the realm of GM foods, where important questions of human and environmental safety are raised, and deep moral anxieties exist, being able to make choices at the point of purchase is of great importance to many people. While almost every opinion poll across the world has indicated that people wish to have information about the means of production using GM, labelling is confined to situations where there are measurable changes in DNA and protein in the final food. Consequently:

- products containing GM soy flour (which may be found in foods such as bread or baby foods) or whole GM soybeans must be labelled with phrases such as *'contains genetically modified soya'* because foreign protein and DNA are present
- products containing derivatives of GM maize (for instance, starch) or GM soybean (for instance, oil or lecithin) will *not* be labelled because protein and DNA are removed during their production. These products

are often found in a whole array of foods including vegetable oils, prepared meals and chocolate.

This position is justified on grounds that there has to be something measurable (that is, foreign DNA or protein) in the final food for labelling to be enforceable and that it is only in this situation that there could conceivably be some health risk that justifies labelling. However, this restriction on the scope of labelling clearly favours the interests of the industry and leave consumers wishing to make their own ethical decisions disadvantaged. A food may not be labelled as 'GM' and a consumer believe it is GM-free, but it could have been produced directly from a GM crop.

The products are not needed

The need for GM herbicide tolerant and insect-resistant crops (which dominate commercial use) is also challenged. The advantages are to farmers (in terms of easier management practices, and claimed environmental benefits are contentious) and to the companies producing the crops. Consumers, who carry the burden of any risks, have no tangible benefit. That GM crops fit into a system of intensive agriculture has also been highlighted, together with the problems that such approaches have brought in the past, such as BSE, antibiotic resistance and loss of farmland wildlife.

Organic agriculture will be a victim

Currently, there is increasing sympathy for organic farming and it has a rapidly increasing market in the UK and the rest of Europe. In the case of genetic modification, genes can be transferred via pollen to pose a new form of contamination for organic farmers' produce. If separation distances between organic and GM fields are not sufficient to prevent gene flow (and pollen can travel large distances on wind and insects), this could threaten organic farmers' livelihoods, because there is an international consensus that the use of genetic modification is not consistent with organic methods of production and its use is not allowed under many national and international standards.

For example, in the EU, a 1999 Regulation[6] states:

> Genetically modified organisms (GMOs) and products derived therefrom are not compatible with the organic production method; in order to maintain consumer confidence in organic production, genetically

modified organisms, parts thereof and products derived therefrom should not be used in products labelled as from organic production.

In the United States, the National Organic Program issued a rule in 2000[7] to implement the Organic Food Production Act of 1990 that uses the term 'excluded methods' to describe products of biotechnology, and prohibits the use of genetically modified organisms and methods in production and handling of organic products.

Beyond Europe and the US, there is no international legal regime, but basic international standards for organic production are agreed and monitored by the International Federation of Organic Agriculture Movements. As with the US and European Rules, the Federation's General Principles provide that

Genetic engineering has no place in organic production and processing,

And the document goes on to state that

Certification bodies / standardising organisations shall set standards and make every effort including relevant documentation to ensure that no genetically engineered organisms or products thereof are used in organic production and processing.[8]

Government is not impartial

Of course, risk assessment and management procedures will never be foolproof whoever is undertaking them, but the public has a right to expect that judgements take the public interest seriously and that the potential for unintended effects is not discounted. That Government and its institutions have become too close to industry and its interests is one strand of the public concern about judgements over safety.

A recent review of public spending on GM food and agriculture bio-technology research concluded that only around 11–16 per cent was on 'safety' of GM crops and foods, the remainder being on research more relevant to development (Barling and Henderson, 2000). This is changing, as a result of questions being asked during the GM furore (announcements have been made in 1999 and 2000 of major research programmes to look at gene flow and impacts of GM crops on biodiversity (Levidow and Carr, 2000b)), but it is clear that tensions exist in the division of research spending intended to support industry and to answer questions of safety – a division which may have been too generous to industry and neglected public concerns. Therefore, the feeling that there has been a rush to commercialise GM crops and foods so that R&D costs can be recouped may not be misplaced and may, indeed, as the commissioning of new research now suggests, have meant that safety was given a back seat in the process, leaving risk assessors and managers ill-equipped to make difficult judgements.

Lack of confidence in the Government to handle the GM risk issues fairly grew as a result of their mishandling of a preliminary research study on the safety of GM potatoes containing an insecticidal protein, called a lectin, from the snowdrop. However, it was not so much the research findings themselves (which were provisional and needed confirmation) but rather the heavy-handed attempts to suppress and discredit them which provoked such an adverse reaction.

In August 1998, in a *World in Action* TV programme, Dr Arpad Pusztai of the Rowett Research Institute revealed that his results suggested that the GM potatoes could impair the growth of and damage the immune system of rats. He was initially hailed as a whistleblower and then rapidly removed from his position, gagged and disgraced, having allegedly misled the public about the implications of his work. He was also prevented from discussing his findings with the audit committee set up to examine the work, which decided it was flawed.

However, in February 1999, a group of international scientists announced their support for Dr Pusztai's work.[9] But in an effort to contain the controversy, rather than funding more research, the Royal Society was enlisted to investigate. Their report, published in May, criticised the design of the Pusztai study and emphasised that new results should not be released until they had been subject to peer review (Royal Society, 1999). Even so, when *The Lancet* published the research in October (Ewan and Pusztai, 1999), following review by six scientists, the majority of whom recommended publication, the Royal Society was not pleased. Richard Horton, the editor of *The Lancet*, was threatened by a senior member of the Royal Society that he would try and have him sacked.[10]

Such an Establishment response was disturbingly reminiscent of the BSE affair and the efforts of Government and scientists to discount the dangers. As a result, the public was left wondering what there was to hide and whether this was another case of collusion between Government and industry – not a good recipe for safety.

Consumers can make a difference

Research conducted in 1996 had shown that people felt powerless to affect the trajectory of GM foods (Grove-White *et al.*, 1997). NGOs managed to develop a campaign that empowered people to make a difference because it was targeted not at the biotechnology industry directly or at politicians, but at the food producers who promised choice. Well informed by the NGOs of the issues at stake, ranging from safety, poor regulations and lack of choice, many individuals contacted food producers and supermarkets and told them they did not want GM foods. Campaigns to boycott certain brands containing GM soybean were launched. Having little or no actual investment in GM crops, but having massive reliance on branding, cumulative individual actions had a massive impact on food producers, who had to go to enormous efforts to remove all GM ingredients (including derivatives) from their products.

The biotechnology industry response

Once it was clear that the future of GM foods in Europe was being threatened, the biotechnology industry was forced to take steps to remedy the situation. Internally, investment in GM was reduced and restructuring of the industry occurred. Interestingly, while Monsanto had always been a major target of the NGOs, the rest of the biotechnology industry also turned on Monsanto, blaming it for arrogance and neglect of public demands for labelling.

Externally, a string of public relations exercises have taken place trying to sell the benefits of GM foods on the one hand and discredit the NGOs on the other hand. For example, the biotechnology industry is now actively promoting the 'second generation' of GM crops. It is claimed that many of these will bring consumer benefits by offering foods with enhanced nutritional value (so-called 'functional foods'). Functional foods are defined as 'foods with ingredients that claim to provide a health benefit to consumers beyond the nutritional benefits ordinarily provided by the foods themselves'.[11] Non-GM functional food products already available include yoghurts with 'bio' cultures, spreads with cholesterol-lowering compounds, bread with fish oil, and soft drinks with added fibre.

The market for functional foods is being developed in response to the growing public interest in the links between diet and health. Foods with enhanced nutritional benefits are seen by companies as a way to achieve added-value growth and profitability in an otherwise highly competitive food market with tight margins and slow-growing food sales. Food companies around the world are restructuring their operations and spending literally hundreds of millions of dollars to develop and market functional food and beverage products (Heasman, 1999). The real value of functional food to companies is not in their potential to improve the health of the nation but in the 'exciting opportunities' functional foods offer 'to food manufacturers and retailers to add value and differentiate their products' (MacKenzie, 1996).

Other genetic modifications to the nutritional composition of crops are intended to facilitate food or animal feed production or provide ingredients for other industrial uses from cosmetics and personal healthcare to biodegradable plastics and bio-fuels.

In terms of discrediting Western NGOs, the industry claims that by obstructing the development of GM crops, the developing world will not be able to feed its growing populations. The industry argument is that the world's population, which is currently about 6 billion, is expected to reach 8 billion by 2020 and 11 billion by 2050[12] and therefore more food will have to be produced. The advocates of genetic engineering believe that the increasing demand for food must be met without expanding the amount of land used for agricultural purposes (to protect biodiversity) and by addressing issues of soil erosion, salinisation, overgrazing and pollution of water supplies (Monsanto, 1997).

Therefore, in its defence, the biotechnology industry has taken upon itself the care of health in the developed world (through functional foods) and feeding the poor and hungry. These are two rather contradictory functions – functional foods will be expensive and available only to a few, and the poor have no purchasing power so are of little interest to the industry. What is striking is how the industry has not engaged seriously with the issues that have been raised about decision making and choice. The only part of the campaign against GM foods that is being replied to is whether they are needed and to do this the industry is cast as the provider of a golden future. This is, of course, a crucial tactic in trying to maintain investor confidence in the genetic bubble, but whether it works in terms of engaging with the underlying issues is more debatable. Overall, it is a very shallow response. The promises of the future are equally contestable in terms of safety and all the other issues raised by the current generation of GM foods still apply. Casting the multinationals behind biotech foods as the defenders of the poor is unlikely to be persuasive in many quarters, especially as the industry insists on patent protection for genes and is developing genetic-use-restriction technologies (such as the Terminator gene) which act against the interests of the poor.

Although it is a very insubstantial response, it is not surprising that the biotechnology industry has continued to adopt a rhetorical role as the golden goose – now just laying slightly different eggs than it did in the mid- to late-1990s. Governance is not industry's role any more than it is that of the NGOs. However, whether GM foods have any future in

Europe will depend on how the decision-making framework evolves and whether it gains public confidence. Industry should consider how its response will affect governance and whether touting promises is really the way to encourage good decision making.

Conclusions

During the late 1990s, the campaign run by NGOs against the introduction of GM foods resonated with public concerns across a whole spectrum of issues. The ability of science to predict adverse consequences in complex risk situations had been undermined through climate change and ozone depletion, among other things. Confidence in institutions to manage risks and act impartially in the public interest had been further eroded by the BSE episode. Increasingly, there was seen to be a linkage between industry and Government that left the public interest marginalised. Governments' views were based upon the assumption that what was good for (big) business was good for the country and this was being questioned. Attitudes to farming and the countryside were also changing, with a growing suspicion of industrial agriculture. The morality of transferring genes between species and where it would all end was also a cause of latent unease.

It was into this context that GM foods were introduced and, in a market economy, trading on choice, denying choice and its legitimacy was a fundamental error by the industry and regulators. The question is, now, how can confidence be restored in the social systems by which decisions on technological trajectories and risk are made? In a plural society, the ways in which these decisions are made will need to be more inclusive. Broader boundaries on what is considered relevant to risk evaluation will be essential. The claim that progress means a certain path and that there are no alternatives will not command respect but be seen as favouring certain interests.

Recently, the UK Government's Agriculture and Environment Biotechnology Commission recognised that scientific findings alone cannot legitimise the commercial growing of GM crops and that there are other issues (including socio-economic and ethical) that have to be taken into account (AEBC, 2001). The European Commission's recently announced consultation 'Towards a strategic vision of life sciences and biotechnology' also recognises the need for a more rounded approach (CEC, 2001).

The challenge for the biotechnology industry is whether it can escape from the model where future products are hailed as the justification for present practices and whether it can enter a more mature debate that recognises the legitimacy of other parties' concerns. If it doesn't, the future for GM crops of any description looks bleak. In taking a new approach, not only will more criteria have to be considered relevant and agreed up front, but comparing options rather than maintaining the pretence that risk assessments can impartially determine whether an action is 'safe' or 'dangerous' will be needed. Techniques such as multi-criteria mapping provide one way of tackling things differently (Stirling and Mayer, 2000).

Notes

1 *See www.greenpeace.org*
2 CEC (1991) and Lex (1995).
3 Biotechnology and the European Public Concerted Action Group (1997).
4 Clydesdale (1996) and Royal Society (1998), Tiede *et al.* (1989).
5 Advisory Committee on Novel Foods and Processes (1994) and Advisory Committee on Releases to the Environment (1997).
6 Council Regulation (EC) No 1804/1999 of 19 July 1999 supplementing Regulation (EEC) No 2092/91 on organic production of agricultural products and indications referring thereto on agricultural products and foodstuffs to include livestock production (OJ L 222, 24.8.1999, p. 1).
7 USDA AMS NOP Final Rule, 21 December, 2000, 7CFR 205.2.
8 OAM Basic Standards for Organic Production and Processing (adopted Basel, 2000: the current draft revision of those standards is in identical terms).
9 'Ousted scientist and the damning research into food safety', *The Guardian*, 12 February 1999.
10 'Pro-GM food scientist "threatened editor"', *The Guardian*, 1 November 1999.
11 International Association of Consumer Food Organizations (1999).
12 Kendall (1997) and Vasil (1998).

References

Advisory Committee on Novel Foods and Processes (1994) *Report on the use of antibiotic resistance markers in genetically modified food organisms*, London: MAFF.

Advisory Committee on Releases to the Environment (1997) *Annual Report No 4: 1996/97*, London: DETR.

AEBC (2001) *Crops on trial*, London: Agriculture and Environment Biotechnology Commission.

Barling, D. and Henderson, R. (2000) *Safety First? A map of public sector research into GM food and food crops in the UK*, Centre for Food Policy, Thames Valley University, London, Discussion paper 12.

Biotechnology and the European Public Concerted Action Group (1997) 'Europe ambivalent on biotechnology', *Nature*, vol. 387, pp. 845–7.

CEC (1991) *Promoting the competitive environment for the industrial activities based on biotechnology within the Community*, Commission Communication to Parliament and the Council, CEC (19) 629 final, Brussels: Commission of the European Communities.

CEC (2001) *Towards a strategic vision of life sciences and biotechnology: consultation document*, Communication from the Commission, COM (2001) 454 final. Brussels: Commission of the European Communities.

Clydesdale, F.M. (ed.) (1996) 'Allergenicity of foods produced by genetic modification', *Food Science and Nutrition*, vol. 36, special supplement.

Ewan, S.W.B. and Pusztai, A. (1999) 'Effect of diets containing genetically modified potatoes expressing *Galanthus nivalis* lectin on rat small intestine', *The Lancet*, vol. 354, pp. 1353–4.

Grove-White, R., Macnaghton, P., Mayer, S. and Wynne, B. (1997) *Uncertain World. Genetically modified organisms: food and public attitudes in Britain*, Lancaster: Centre for the Study of Environmental Change.

Hamstra, A.M. (1995) *Consumer Acceptance Model for Food Biotechnology. Final Report*, The Netherlands: SWOKA, Institute for Consumer Research.

Heasman, M. (1999) 'The Functional Foods Revolution', in *Future Food*, London: The Caroline Walker Trust.

International Association of Consumer Food Organizations (1999) *Functional Foods – Public Health Boon or 21st Century Quackery?*, London: The International Association of Consumer Food Organizations.

Kendall, H.W., Beachy, R., Eisner, T., Gould, F., Herdt, R., Raven, P.H., Schell, J.S. and Swaminathan, M.S. (1997) *Bioengineering of crops: report of the World Bank Panel on Transgenic Crops*, Washington, DC: World Bank.

Levidow, L. (1994) 'Biotechnology regulation as symbolic normalisation' *Technology Analysis and Strategic Management*, vol. 6, no. 3, pp. 273–88.

Levidow, L. and Carr, S. (2000a) 'UK: precautionary commercialization?', *Journal of Risk Research*, vol. 3, pp. 261–70.

Levidow, L. and Carr, S. (2000b) Environmental precaution as learning: GM crops in the UK, in *Cow up a tree: Learning and knowledge for change in agriculture: Case Studies from Industrialised Countries*, pp. 323–35, LEARN Group, ed. M. Cerf, D. Gibbon, B. Hubert, R. Ison, J. Jiggins, M. Paine, J. Proost, N. Röling, Versailles: INRA.

Lex, M. (1995) 'Promoting the competitiveness of biotechnology in Europe'. *Trends in Biotechnology*, vol. 13, pp. 39–40.

Lutman, P.J.W. (1999) *BCPC Symposium Proceedings No. 72: Gene flow and its consequences for GM oilseed rape. Farnham, Surrey: British Crop Protection Council*.

MacKenzie, D. (1996) 'Functional claims – opportunity or minefield?', *Low & Lite Digest*, no. 3, March.

Millstone, E., Brunner E. and Mayer, S. (1999) 'Beyond 'substantial equivalence'', *Nature*, vol. 401, pp. 525–6.

Monsanto (1997) *Report on Sustainable Development including Environmental, Safety and Health Performance*, St Louis, Missouri: Monsanto.

Medical Research Council (2000) *Report of an MRC working group on genetically modified (GM) foods* London: Medical Research Council.

Royal Commission on Environmental Pollution (1989) *The Release of Genetically Engineered Organisms into the Environment*, London: HMSO.

Royal Society (1998) *Genetically modified plants for food use*, London: Royal Society.

Royal Society (1999) *Review of data on possible toxicity of GM potatoes, 17 May 1999*, London: Royal Society.

Royal Society of Canada (2001) *Elements of Precaution: Recommendations for the Regulation of Food Biotechnology in Canada*, Toronto: Royal Society of Canada.

Stirling, A. and Mayer, S. (2000) 'Precautionary risk appraisal of a genetically modified crop', *International Journal of Occupational Health and Environmental Medicine*, vol. 6, no. 4, pp. 296–311.

Tiede, J.M., Colwell, R.K., Grossman, Y.L., Hodson, R.E., Kenski, R.E., Mack, R.N. and Regal, P.J. (1989) 'The planned introduction of genetically engineered organisms: ecological considerations and recommendations.' *Ecology*, vol. 70, pp. 298–315.

Vasil, I.K. (1998) 'Biotechnology and food security for the 21st century: a real-world perspective', *Nature Biotechnology*, vol. 16, pp. 399–400.

Comments by Peter Siddall

You will be relieved to know that I do not disagree with everything in Sue Mayer's paper! We do need an informed and balanced debate about this important technology. Speaking as a non-scientist, I have an opportunity to respond in a broader way. I am Chairman of Horticulture Research International (HRI) which is sponsored by DEFRA and is the UK's largest horticultural R&D organisation. HRI employs 450 scientists in the UK, many of whom have excellent global reputations in the field of biotechnology. I am not one of them – I do not know my genomics from my proteomics, but it is clear that there is more to this question than excellent science.

I would like to provide some additional facts so that there can be a more balanced discussion. I want to make three points at the start:

- Firstly, this is a global question not purely an issue for the UK and Europe; there are many parts of the world that take a different view, and I mention US and China specifically
- Secondly, world hunger is a major problem for us all, which will become much worse in the future
- Thirdly, no technology is risk free, even kitchen knives!

I have three primary sources of information: the ISAAA (The Information Service for the Acquisition of Agri-Biotech Applications) from Ithaca, NY, with data and comments from its director, Dr Clive James; the Head of Plant Sciences, University of Oxford, Professor Chris Leaver; and the EC Consultation Paper 'Towards a Strategic Vision of Life Sciences and Biotechnology'.[1]

According to ISAAA, the global area of transgenic crops will reach 50 million hectares in 2001 – that is a 10 per cent increase on 2000. Millions of farmers, large and small, in developing and developed countries, choose to continue to increase their plantings year by year. The total acreage planted since 1996 is now 175 million ha (about 400 million acres). If you think about that in terms of food produced and meals consumed, it is a daunting figure.

The benefits that people (farmers in particular) cite for this are:

- sustainable, resource-efficient practices, including, specifically, lower energy, better moisture utilisation, less soil erosion

- less spraying means a reduced health hazard (particularly for people in the developing world who are not wearing protective clothing during spraying) together with reduced harmful residues which contaminate the environment
- Safer food and animal feed from these products.

Clive James concludes

> Governments, supported by the global scientific and international development community, must ensure the continued safe and effective testing and introduction of GM crops and implement regulatory programmes that inspire public confidence.

Some more data from ISAAA.[2] Figure 3.1 shows that in 2000, when this chart was produced, 45 million acres were planted. The total for 2001 is 50 million ha – up another 10 per cent in total. By country, USA tops the list while Argentina and Canada are both very significant. In the period 1997–99, China has officially introduced 23 different types of GM crops for commercial production. Figure 3.2 shows the global area of transgenic plantings, crop by crop. You may be interested that soyabean is the largest at over 26 million ha, followed by maize (10 million ha), with cotton (5 million ha) and canola (3 million ha).

In a recent lecture entitled: 'Food for Thought – doing nothing is not an option',[3] Professor Chris J. Leaver, Head of Plant Sciences, Oxford University, made the following statements:

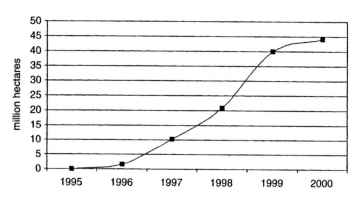

Figure 3.1 Global area under transgenic crops.

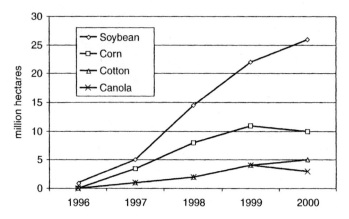

Figure 3.2   Global area under transgenic crops (by crop).

- More than 15 per cent of the world population at this moment are undernourished
- Malnutrition is the major cause of death in the world today
- Of the 12 million children that are dying under the age of five at the moment, 50 per cent are attributable to malnutrition
- World population is 6 billion today, and expected to increase by 50 per cent in the next 50 years
- China has 25 per cent of the world population and 7 per cent of the farmland.

He believes that in order to achieve better standards, and sustainable food production, we will require double and triple the food production that we have today – a huge challenge. He says 'the application of plant biotechnology together with conventional plant breeding and improved agricultural practices may provide solution to some of the challenges'. Of the present situation of GM plants, he says 'the manner of the introduction of these new technologies was over enthusiastic and lacked awareness of cultural sensitivities, which has led to widespread loss of community confidence, that has in turn been exploited by non-representative groups and activists for their own political ends'.

He concludes

If we are to satisfy the real and legitimate environmental concerns associated with modern high input agriculture and the threat of global warming and still feed the increasing population in a sustainable manner, we must assume the responsibility for fully evaluating this technology to contribute to the security of future generations.

The European Commission's current consultation paper, recently released, is called 'Towards a Strategic Vision of Life Sciences and Biotechnology'. The EC says

> Life sciences and biotechnology have entered a stage of exponential growth, opening up vast potential to move economies in Europe and globally towards more sustainable development and improved quality of life. They are therefore of strategic importance in Europe's quest to become a leading knowledge-based economy. Europe cannot afford to miss the opportunity that these new sciences and technologies offer. We therefore need to address all the relevant questions, including where necessary broader and generic issues.

It also states that 'A main challenge will be to ensure that innovation successfully transforms research and inventions into viable new products and services.'

The EC states that despite increasing concerns about potential risks *no peer-reviewed scientific evidence exists for any adverse effects to human health or the environment of the GMOs which have so far been authorised for marketing.*

And, finally, on the ethical implications, the EC consultation paper proposes that 'we need to identify, and even anticipate, the ethical issues, provide focused advice on the often technically complex matters, and make available relevant factors and facilitate societal scrutiny and debate'.

That is what I believe should be happening now. We must reduce the rhetoric and draw back from damaging confrontation. All parties must work together systematically and constructively to address people's concerns, we must evaluate, test and put to work this powerful technology for the good of present and future generations. The evidence is that the developing world must act quickly.

Notes

1 Towards a strategic vision of life sciences and biotechnology consultation document, COM (2001) 454 final, Brussels, Commission of the European Communities.
2 Global Review of Commercialised Transgenic Crops: 2000, ISAAA, Ithaca New York, available at *www.isaaa.org*
3 British Crop Protection Council, Bawden Lecture, 2001, available at *www.bcpc.org*

4

Child Labour in the Third World

Andrew Clayton

Introduction

Over the past decade, child labour in the Third World has received increasing attention from many different organisations, including human-rights groups, development agencies, governments, trade unions, UN agencies and the private sector. There has also been greater consumer awareness of child labour and many multinational companies have been under pressure from consumers to ensure that their products have not been produced with child labour. Various actions have been taken by companies to eradicate or minimise child labour in supply chains. Some have undoubtedly had positive benefits for children, and others have been harmful to children. This chapter reviews these experiences and draws out lessons and recommendations for companies in responding to child labour. One of the basic premises of this paper, however, is that any attempt by businesses to eradicate child labour in their factories and supply chains must recognise the wider problem of child labour in the countries in which they work.

In most developing countries, less than 5 per cent of child labourers work in the export sector.[1] Most children work in agriculture, as domestic workers, in the informal economy or in the production or manufacture of commodities for domestic markets rather than for export. Furthermore, working conditions are often far worse for such children compared to those working in the export sector. The important point here is not that child labour in the export sector is in any way acceptable, but rather that the demand for cheap labour by multinational companies has not created the problem of child labour but has instead exploited an existing problem. Dismissing child labourers from factories does not solve the problem of child labour but may force children to seek other sources of employment in potentially more harmful conditions. If companies are genuinely concerned about children's welfare and not just about their reputation as an ethical company, they need to develop more sophisticated approaches based on a deeper understanding of the causes of child labour and a recognition of the respective roles of governments, trade unions and NGOs (non-governmental organisations).

The next section analyses the general problem of child labour in developing countries. This provides the necessary context for the second section on the responsibilities of the private sector in relation to child labour.

Christian Aid was one of the first NGOs to campaign against child labour. Since 1989, it has supported the South Asia Coalition Against Child Servitude (SACCS), which has led a campaign to rescue children from bonded labour in India. More recently, Christian Aid has supported a number of initiatives against child labour, including the Global March Against Child Labour, the Rugmark Initiative which sought to eliminate child labour from the carpet industry in South Asia, and the campaign against the use of children in the manufacture of footballs in India (*see* Christian Aid 1994, 1997). These campaigns have all played an important role in raising the problem of child labour among the general public, the media, the private sector and governments. Of particular note is the central role that the Global March Against Child Labour played in lobbying the International Labour Organisation to adopt Convention 182 on The Worst Forms of Child Labour in 1999.[2]

Child labour: an overview

What is child labour?

Not all work is harmful to children. Work has, under certain circumstances, the potential to bring many positive benefits to children. Work can be an integral part of the child's development, teaching skills which will be of great benefit later in life. For many poor households, children can make a valuable contribution to family income. Work can also help teach children to develop a sense of responsibility to others. Yet work can also have extremely negative effects on children.

A distinction is sometimes made between child 'work' and child 'labour'; the former refers to work carried out by children which is not harmful to them, the latter refers to harmful, hazardous and exploitative forms of work. However, in many situations it is very difficult to define precisely which types of work are harmful to a child and which are not. Take, for example, children in rural communities who assist their families in agricultural work. Assisting parents in agricultural tasks is essential if children are to learn to farm themselves later. In many places, the demand for extra labour at certain points in the agricultural calendar means that families are dependent on children at these times. The issue is one of degree: help with planting or harvesting at certain points in the year, or light daily tasks such as milking are activities which need not be detrimental to children's development, and may bring many positive benefits to the child. Yet heavy manual work, or working such long hours that the child has neither the time nor the energy to attend school or to play, are likely to be damaging to the child's development.

In addition to the tasks undertaken, the working conditions must also be taken into consideration. For example, many children in India are employed in the manufacture of *beedis*, a local cigarette. The actual work of rolling a cigarette is a light task, but when a child has to make *beedis* for long hours, crouched on the floor with poor light and ventilation, and with an abusive employer, such work is likely to be physically and emotionally harmful (Human Rights Watch, 1995). Similarly, helping with domestic tasks such as cooking and cleaning becomes harmful when, for example, the child is working very long hours so that schooling suffers, or if the child works in a household where they are subject to physical or sexual abuse.

It is more helpful to think of child labour as a continuum; at one end there are the most harmful and dangerous types of work done by children; at the other end there are types of work that are neither exploitative nor detrimental to children. In between there are types of work that are not in themselves necessarily harmful but can be so under certain conditions. Thus, it is not possible to generalise about such work as being harmful or not, since the effects of such work on children must be assessed in each context.

Some types of work, such as child slavery, child prostitution, or working in dangerous environments or with hazardous chemicals, are without question extremely harmful in all contexts. In relation to these types of work, steps must be taken immediately to end such practices. Any type of work that is hazardous to a child can never be in the 'child's best interest'. NGOs like Christian Aid are focusing on programmes that target the elimination of the worst forms of child labour, as defined in International Labour Organisation's Convention 182 and its Recommendation 190.

There are other, less harmful types of child labour – such as working as a waiter in a tea shop or as a street vendor – which are not covered in ILO Convention 182. While ideally such children should be in school, eliminating this type of work generally requires a more gradual approach from NGOs. Removing children from the workplace in such situations is not always in their best interest. A better approach to promoting the rights of working children can be through improving the conditions in which they work and providing them with schooling which meets the special needs of working children. Alternative sources of income must also be found for families dependent on the income generated by children.

The causes of child labour

The reasons why children work are complex, diverse and context-specific. In each context there is a unique range of factors that have denied children their basic rights. Consequently there are no simple, universal solutions to removing children from exploitative and dangerous types of work. It is therefore essential that careful social and economic research is carried out by NGOs, governmental bodies and companies before intervening. Unless the reasons why children work are understood, any solutions may, at best, be of little help and, at worst, make the situation even more harmful to children (Boyden *et al.*, 1998).

It is widely recognised that poverty is the most fundamental cause of child labour. Most of the worst cases of child labour involve children from poor families in developing countries. Children work when their parents have insufficient income and resources to provide their families with their basic needs. Providing secure employment and decent wages for adults is essential if poor families are to be no longer dependent on the income from their children. To eliminate child labour in the long term, it is therefore necessary to break the cycle of poverty that underlies much child labour and means that children of former child labourers often end up as child labourers themselves. Many child labourers grow up illiterate, unskilled and with serious health problems. As a consequence, many of them are unable to support their own families in adulthood, so their own children may get drawn into work to support the family. The provision of free, universal good quality and compulsory education is also of critical importance in eradicating child labour in the long term. Education provides an alternative activity to work, can challenge accepted notions among children and parents about the consequences of child labour and, in the long term, can improve the opportunities for children when they grow up to earn better incomes and break the poverty cycle (Anker, 2000).

Poverty is not the only explanation. Other factors play a significant role. Social differentiation within societies – gender, class, ethnicity and caste – can all be critical in influencing which children are most vulnerable to exploitation.[3] In India, for example, the majority of child labourers are 'Dalits' (the untouchables in the Hindu caste system). The discrimination, marginalisation and impoverishment of Dalits in India means that Dalit children are particularly vulnerable to extreme forms of exploitation, such as bonded labour (Thorat, 1999). Family structures, cultural values and attitudes towards education are also important factors. In sub-Saharan Africa, the impact of HIV/AIDS has also changed patterns of child work in places where there have been high mortality rates among the economically active adult population.

Children in urban settings are often vulnerable to different forms of exploitation than those in rural communities. Also, within the same community, some children may be at more risk than others. For example, children from single-parent households may be under more pressure to work than those in which both parents are present, and children from large families more likely to work than those from smaller families. Even within the same household, older children may be under more pressure to work than younger children, and girls expected to work more than their brothers (or vice versa in some societies).

Different societies also have different notions of childhood. For many societies, the idea that childhood should be a time for education and play is quite alien. Many see work as a central part of childhood and as a means by which children learn the skills they need in adult life. This is the reality in many developing countries. This implies that measures which seek to remove children from exploitative labour need to recognise the importance of work in many societies to both adults and the children themselves. Unless alternative forms of work are found that are not exploitative and detrimental to their education and health, children are likely to return to exploitative forms of child labour.

One of the key principles of the Convention on the Rights of the Child – children's participation in decisions that affect them – is crucial in understanding the causes of child labour. If children are to benefit from initiatives to remove them from harmful work places, or improve the conditions within which they work, such initiatives must be based on children's perceptions of work and on what changes they would like to see. This may throw up challenging and discomforting views: many studies have found that children want to continue to work, usually because they or their families are dependent on their income, but also because they may find school of little value. When asked, children often say they prefer to work for an employer for money and enjoy the camaraderie of working with other children rather than working at home, where they may be alone, subject to abuse and receive no payment for their work. And while no child is likely to say that they want to continue working in a harmful environment, many may feel they have no alternative because of the lack of other income-generating activities. Children from poor households may think that not working is simply not a real option, and continue to undertake harmful work if they have no other options. This presents very real challenges for organisations which support children's rights (Green, 1998).

International conventions on protecting children from exploitation

While there are no universal solutions to combating child labour, International human-rights instruments have a crucial role in setting standards for what is and what is not acceptable practice in relation to the employment of children. Three international conventions that have been passed by UN bodies are of particular importance:

1973   Convention on the Minimum Age (ILO no. 138)
1989   UN Convention on the Rights of the Child
1999   Convention on the Worst forms of Child Labour (ILO no. 182)

These will be discussed chronologically. The Minimum Age Convention (no. 138) was adopted by the International Labour Organisation in 1973. The main requirement of this convention is that ratifying it must establish a minimum age for children to work. This covers all forms of economic activity, not just waged employment, although work on small family farms, domestic work in the household and educational work are excluded. The minimum age must be higher than the age children are required to be in school, but the convention states that this should be no lower than 15 years. Provision is made for a temporary minimum age of 14 years in underdeveloped countries. However, the convention sets 18 years as the minimum age for hazardous work, while allowing light, part-time work at 13 years, or 12 years in underdeveloped countries. By February 2002, 116 countries had ratified this convention.

ILO Convention 138 is a particularly important convention in the context of industrialisation and the growth of formal employment, and is therefore directly applicable to multinational companies operating in developing countries. This will be discussed further in the next section. There are some limitations with Convention 138 in relation to relevance and enforcement outside the formal sector. Most child labour takes place on small family farms or within the household – which are exempt from the convention – or in the informal sector – where enforcement is very difficult. In other words, while Convention 138 is crucial for the formal sector, it does not in itself provide an adequate legislative framework for addressing the wider problem of child labour.

The Convention on the Rights of the Child (CRC) provides a much broader international legal framework for the promotion and protection of children's rights. A convention on child rights had been called for in 1978 but there then followed a ten-year period of drafting the text, a process that not only involved governments but also a significant involvement of civil society. The text was unanimously adopted by the UN General Assembly in November 1989. By September 1990, 20 governments had already ratified the convention, which meant the CRC then formally entered international law. By the end of that year, a third of all countries ratified the convention and, by 1995, it had been ratified by nearly 90 per cent of all countries. Now only two countries, the USA and Somalia, have not ratified it. The CRC sets out a clear vision for children's rights and on the obligations of governments to ensure that the rights of children are protected and promoted. In ratifying the CRC, a government commits itself to these obligations and accepts participation in an international monitoring system by which it is held accountable. One of the key challenges for governments in ratifying the CRC is to introduce domestic legislation that is compatible with the demands of the CRC although progress on this has been much slower (Save the Children, 2000a).

The CRC is based on four fundamental principles:

- there must be no discrimination of any kind against any child, such as on grounds of gender, ethnicity, caste, religion or race
- the best interests of the child must be the primary consideration in all decisions affecting children
- the survival and development of the child must be ensured; every child has the inherent right to life and to education
- the views of the child must be taken into account in any decisions that affect him/her, the views of the child being given due weight in accordance with the age and maturity of the child.

Any action affecting children must be based on these principles. Although these principles are open to interpretation, they do set out a basic framework for protecting children's rights.

The CRC also explicitly addresses the issue of child labour in Article 32:

> State parties recognise the right of the child to be protected from economic exploitation and from performing any work that is likely to be hazardous or to interfere with the child's education, or to be harmful to the child's health and physical, mental, spiritual, moral or social development.

This is expanded in Article 34 against sexual exploitation, in Article 35 on the sale, trafficking and abduction of children, and in Article 36 which states 'State parties shall protect the child against all other forms of exploitation prejudicial to any aspects of the child's welfare'. The CRC is not against all forms of child work but focuses on those that are damaging to children. What is particularly important about the CRC in relation to child labour is that the four fundamental principles in the CRC must be adhered to in any intervention to end child labour.

A further ILO Convention complements the CRC and Minimum Age Convention by focusing on protecting children from the most exploitative, damaging and dangerous forms of work. Convention 182 Concerning the Prohibition and Immediate Action For the Elimination of the Worst Forms of Child Labour was passed by the ILO in 1999. This is more specific than the CRC and ILO Convention 138, and has also brought a new urgency to combating the worst forms of child labour, an urgency which is lacking in the CRC.

Convention 182 identifies the following as the worst forms of child labour which require immediate action (Article 3):

- all forms of slavery or practices similar to slavery such as the sale and trafficking of children, debt bondage and serfdom and forced or compulsory recruitment of children for use in armed conflict
- prostitution or pornography
- illicit activities
- work which ... will harm health, safety or morals of children.

In the accompanying Recommendation (no. 190) to the Convention, those states which have ratified the Convention are asked to consider the following as hazardous to children:

- work which exposes children to physical, psychological or sexual abuse
- work underground, underwater, at dangerous heights or in confined spaces

- work with dangerous machinery, equipment and tools, or that involves manual handling or transport of heavy loads
- work in an unhealthy environment which may, for example, expose children to hazardous substances, agents or processes, or to temperatures, noise levels, or vibrations damaging to their health
- work under particularly difficult conditions, such as work for long hours or during the night or work where the child is unreasonably confined to the premises of the employer.

These international conventions – the CRC and ILO Conventions 138 and 182 – provide clear obligations to states about eliminating exploitative child labour. In particular, ILO Convention 182 provides more clarity about what actually constitutes the worst forms of child labour, while the CRC provides the fundamental principles that must be applied if children's rights are to be respected. Together, they provide a strong legal framework for protecting children from the worst forms of child labour. States that ratify these conventions are subject to inspection and monitoring procedures administered by UN bodies and can be held accountable to international law for failure to implement the requirements set out in the conventions. They are also obliged to introduce national legislation that enforces compliance with the standards agreed in these conventions.

Overall strategies for action

There has been an intensive campaign by the ILO, trade unions and NGOs to pressurise governments to ratify Convention 182. By February 2002, and less than three years since the ILO adopted the convention, 116 countries had already ratified the convention. It has taken nearly 30 years for the ILO convention 138 to get this many ratifications. In relation to those governments that have ratified them, NGOs also have an important role in monitoring how they have implemented conventions, such as the introduction of national legislation which outlaws the worst forms of child labour and by establishing an inspectorate to ensure companies are adhering to the conventions.[4]

However, while introducing new legislation is essential in establishing a legal framework for combating child labour, it is not in itself enough. The enforcement of legislation to prohibit child labour must actually protect children. The danger is that legislation can end up penalising or criminalising them, leaving them even more vulnerable to abuse. If children are to be removed from the workplace, then alternative sources of livelihood for them and their families must be found. Otherwise, children may need to seek alternative sources of work. Often this is in the informal economy, where regulation by the state is more difficult and where working conditions may be far worse than in the formal sector. Over the past decade, many well-meaning initiatives to remove children from the workplace have failed because little analysis was made of why children were engaged in such exploitative forms of work. Talking with children about their needs, fears, hopes and desires is also essential for identifying effective strategies. While ensuring that children participate in the decisions that affect them is a basic principle of the Convention on the Rights of the Child, nevertheless, in some situations, there is a potential conflict between the views of the child on the one hand and the protection and development of the child on the other. This is particularly the case with young children who may be unaware of the hazardous nature of their work or the long-term impact of such work on their health, such as working with toxic chemicals. The CRC states that the weight given to the child's view depends on age and maturity. In such situations, it is still important that the views of the child be heard, but adults will need to judge what is in the best interests of the child when it comes to devising strategies for action.

Child labour also has an impact on the adult labour market. Children can be more easily exploited than adults and may be prepared to work for less money. Not only does this deny work opportunities to adults, but can lead to a lowering of the general rates of pay in the sectors in which children work. This can keep poor families in poverty if it means adult family members have no access to secure forms of employment or livelihood. Tackling child labour through improving employment opportunities and conditions for adults is a long-term measure, although child protection and child development must take precedence over concerns about the impact of child labour on the adult labour market.

The complexity of the problem of child labour needs addressing at different levels. High profile campaigns such as the Global March Against Child Labour have played a critical role in changing international law and raising global awareness of the problem of child labour. The Global March was an initiative of a long-term Christian Aid partner, the South Asia Coalition Against Child Servitude, and was launched in January 1998. It developed into an international movement of over 1400 social organisations in 144 countries campaigning for the end of child labour. The Global March played a key role in mobilising public pressure on the member governments of the ILO to adopt Convention 182 on the worst forms of child labour in 1999. These campaigns have taken uncompromising positions in lobbying governments to introduce strong legislation to protect children from exploitation. Changing international and national legislation to provide greater protection to children is essential if the worst forms of child labour are to be eliminated.

It is essential that governments implement tough measures to protect children, but civil society organisations play a crucial role in more localised, grassroots initiatives that directly support working children. Such initiatives involve seeking alternative sources of income, and providing education and health care for working children. Sometimes the approach requires efforts to improve the conditions within which children work. It is essential to protect children who undertake tasks that are not in themselves harmful, but where the conditions are harmful, removing them from the workplace may not always be the best way of helping. A more realistic means of protecting children in the short term may be to improve working conditions by reducing children's hours, establish a better environment at the work place and ensure that employers follow agreed codes of conduct in their treatment of children.

In some contexts, there are good reasons to take a stronger approach against child labour. There may be extreme cases, notably bonded child labour or enslavement, where immediate action must be taken to remove children from the workplace. In India, for example, Christian Aid supports local organisations that have taken an uncompromising stand against bonded child labour and physically rescued children from bonded labour workplaces. Although recognising that bonded labour is rooted in the Indian caste system and poverty, partners argue that taking a more liberal, gradualist approach to child labour in this context is to accept the status quo in which millions of children, especially from lower caste or 'Dalit' families, work in conditions similar to slavery. Yet removing children is not enough; they need support to rehabilitate them back into their communities, or education and alternative sources of livelihood. Rescuing children should always be only part of a broader, long-term programme of tackling the causes of bonded labour and enslavement.

Child labour in the export sector: the role of international companies

This section looks at the specific problem of child labour in the production of goods for export and reviews recent initiatives to address the problem. Much progress has been made by companies to tackle child labour and there is now far more awareness of the issue than a decade ago. However, the complex nature of child labour presents many challenges to companies in eradicating child labour from their supply chains if they are genuinely to put the best interests of children first. Companies clearly have crucial roles to play, but also need to accept that to be effective in ending child labour, they have to work with government and civil society and recognise the wider causes of child labour in the countries in which they operate.

One of the key ethical decisions that companies need to take is over standards. Many countries do not have adequate legislation to protect children from exploitation and there may be social acceptance of young children working long hours. Multinational companies can exploit this and follow local practice, concealing local employment conditions from consumers. However, a basic ethical position is to accept the standards set out in international conventions, notably ILO Conventions 138 and 182. Companies that engage in international trade and claim to be socially responsible have an ethical obligation to enforce these international standards, even if local employers in the countries in which they work fall far short of these standards. These standards have been agreed by the international community through the UN system and provide a benchmark of minimum standards in relation to the employment of all those below 18 years old.

However, it should be noted that these international conventions hold governments to account and cannot be legally forced on companies unless there is subsequent national legislation on these standards in place in the country of operation.

While there should be no new recruitment of children in breach of these international conventions, the difficult issue facing companies is how to act when they find that there are children working either directly for them or in the manufacture or production of commodities that they buy. Few multinational companies would now wish to suffer the bad publicity that is likely to follow should they be found to be directly employing children. In the early 1990s, campaign groups and the media in Europe and North America began to raise public awareness about the involvement of child labour in the production of consumer goods. Consumer boycotts were organised to target companies that were known to be exploiting child labour. These included campaigns on carpets from India, sports goods from Pakistan and garments from Bangladesh.

In response, many companies took drastic action to eradicate child labour by sacking all those felt to be underage. Similar action was taken when Senator Harkin introduced the US *Child Labour Deterrence Bill* in 1992 calling for a prohibition on the import to the US of any goods in which children under 15 years old were involved in production.

Although the Bill has never become law, the threat of the ban led to the sacking of an estimated 55 000 child workers in the Bangladesh garment industry. Rather than protecting children, this caused great damage. The families dependent on the income of these children became more impoverished and many of those who found alternative jobs ended up undertaking far more dangerous and harmful forms of work than their previous employment in the garment industry.

Such actions failed to recognise the broader context of child labour and consequently failed to put the welfare of the child workers first. Since then, other initiatives in which there is greater recognition of children's best interests have been developed collaboratively between companies and NGOs in an attempt to take a more responsible approach to ending child labour. Two of the most common approaches are labelling systems, and rehabilitation and education programmes.

One of the earliest and best known labelling initiatives was Rugmark. This was established in 1994 in order to eliminate the illegal use of child labour in the carpet industry in South Asia. The Rugmark Foundation has established a system of labelling carpets that guarantees that they are free of child labour. Manufacturers and exporters in India and Nepal make commitments not to use child labour, and importers in Europe and the US commit themselves to purchasing only carpets with the Rugmark label. Carpet exporters pay 0.25 per cent of the export value of their carpets to Rugmark and importers contribute 1 per cent of the import value of the carpets. These contributions are used to carry out inspections of looms to ensure that no child labour is used, and to set up schools and rehabilitation centres for former child labourers. By February 2000, 216 carpet exporters in India were licensed with Rugmark (out of a total of approximately 2700 exporters), and over 1.5 million carpets had been exported from India. During this period, inspections found 1297 children working on looms, and the carpet manufacturers responsible for these looms had their Rugmark licence withdrawn immediately (Boyden *et al.*, 1998, p. 310).

Although less than 10 per cent of carpet exporters in India are licensed with Rugmark, Rugmark's achievements have been considerable. It has led to the removal of children from harmful work in the carpet industry and provided education and rehabilitation. Furthermore, although the number of children directly assisted by Rugmark is a small proportion of the total number of children working in the carpet industry, Rugmark has had a much wider impact. The labelling programme and international campaign has created much greater awareness about child labour in the carpet industry in governments, NGOs, the private sector and with consumers. The Indian Government has now targeted the carpet industry in its National Child Labour Project and there are a number of other initiatives involving industry and NGOs (Ravi, 2001).

There are, however, a number of limitations with Rugmark and labelling schemes in general. Firstly, it is very difficult adequately to monitor all the looms on which carpets carrying the Rugmark label are produced. Secondly, it is not clear whether or not the provision of education and rehabilitation schemes for former child labourers is adequate compensation for the loss of income from their work in carpet industry. If not, they are likely to seek alternative sources of work which may be no less harmful than in the carpet industry. Perhaps the most important limitation of labelling is that it does not address the structural reasons for the employment of children in the carpet industry. Carpet manufacture in India is a cottage industry carried out by individual loom owners spread over hundreds of villages in Uttar Pradesh. Loom owners weave carpets themselves or hire labour to do so and then the carpets are sold through a series of sub-contractors and intermediaries before being exported. It is estimated that loom owners receive as little as 10 per cent of the export price of a carpet. There is, thus, a major incentive for loom owners to employ children who will work for lower wages in order for loom owners to increase their profits. Unless exporters are willing to set up alternative supply structures with fewer intermediaries and ensure that loom owners get a better price for their carpets, there will continue to be a strong demand for child labour in the carpet industry.

Another approach to child labour in the production of consumer goods for export has been to establish a process of phased transition to end child labour. One of the best known cases of this has been in football production in Sialkot, Pakistan, where up to three-quarters of the world's hand-stitched footballs are produced. The use of child labour in football production in Sialkot was taken up by pressure groups and trade unions in Europe and America in the mid-1990s. In response, many of the sports goods industries wanted to ban immediately all child labour in the production of their footballs. Yet, had this happened, many of the children working on football production would have moved to far more harmful work, such as making surgical implements. Save the Children visited Sialkot in 1996 with the World Federation of Sporting Goods Industries to identify how child labour in football production could be phased out in a more responsible manner that put child welfare first. Following on from this, in February 1997 Save the Children, ILO, UNICEF and the Sialkot Chamber of Commerce and Industry signed a partnership agreement to set up a programme which had five main components: education; credit and savings; awareness raising; social monitoring; and formal monitoring. Local football manufacturers could choose to join the programme, and sports goods companies could commit themselves to using only suppliers who joined the programme.[5]

The programme has helped an estimated 40000 children. By December 1999, 35 new schools had been established, the infrastructure of 139 schools had been improved and 517 teachers had been trained. The credit and savings scheme was implemented to provide alternative sources of income to families of child labourers, while UNICEF undertook a programme to raise the awareness among communities of the potentially harmful effect of child labour. Save the Children has also undertaken a long-term study to assess the impact of the programme and monitor its effect on children's lives. ILO has taken responsibility for the formal monitoring of child labour by funding inspectors to ensure that no children under 14 are working in the football stitching centres (Save the Children, 2000b). Of the 68 football manufacturers in Sialkot making top-grade footballs for export, 36 have joined the programme, and 58 international brands have committed themselves to using only manufacturers who have joined the programme.

The Sialkot programme provides a good example of a successful programme to phase out child labour and to provide education and alternative sources of income. Save the Children believes that this has been a successful kind of partnership involving the private sector, government, donors and NGOs, and that the same approach needs to be applied to other industries, especially those involving more harmful types of child labour.[6] However, to make such partnerships effective requires commitment and resources from all parties. As with Rugmark, mechanisms need to be developed so that the private sector contributes towards the educational and rehabilitation aspects of the programmes.

Another approach adopted by many companies is to establish their own codes of conduct in relation to child labour. As with other initiatives to end the exploitation of children, these can be very effective if carefully developed and implemented, but in many cases they are of little value and even potentially harmful to working children if ill-conceived or poorly monitored. Codes of conduct must put the best interests of children first and companies need to examine thoroughly how codes of conduct can achieve this.

Nowadays, most of the well known 'High Street' brands have their own codes of conduct and their websites proudly proclaim that their products have not been made by children. But if a company's code of conduct is to have a genuine impact on protecting children from economic exploitation rather than being merely a public relations exercise aimed at concerned consumers, then certain practices must be followed. One key issue is whether or not a code of conduct has been adopted unilaterally by a company or been developed through negotiation with trade unions and NGOs.[7] Such negotiation is necessary to overcome some of the limitations commonly found in company codes of conduct. There are three main areas of concern with codes of conduct (Anti-slavery International, 1996).

First, to be effective they must give precise and measurable standards in relation to the employment of children. If the code of conduct merely gives broad general commitments, then it becomes very difficult to implement. The international labour standards as set out in ILO conventions provide the benchmark for codes of conduct and in relation to child labour this means Conventions 138 and 182.[8] As a minimum, codes of conduct must require companies to ensure that neither they nor those in their supply chain are in breach of ILO conventions 138 and 182, or any relevant national legislation on the employment of children. Although the relevance and enforceability of the Minimum Age Convention 138 is difficult to enforce in the informal sector, it is aimed primarily at formal employment, and multinational companies are in a position to ensure that this convention is followed. There may still be problems in identifying the precise age of a worker in the absence of a national system of birth certificates, although approximate assessments can probably be made in most cases. Thus, no companies should employ children full-time under the age of 15 years, or for a temporary period only, under 14 years in underdeveloped countries. However, for hazardous work the convention sets 18 years as the minimum age. Children can be given light, part-time work at 13 years, or 12 years in underdeveloped countries. No child of 11 years or younger should be employed at all in a commercial environment. There is less clarity as to what actually constitutes full-time work and what constitutes part-time work but codes of conduct need to give precise working hours and holiday allowances for both full- and part-time work. In setting working hours, companies need to follow the overall aim of the convention to protect children, rather than exploit the lack of precision in the convention to impose long hours on 'part-time' child workers. Companies should also enforce a ban on anyone under 18 years old undertaking work that is prohibited under the ILO Convention 182 on the worst forms of child labour.

A second concern is that while the company may adopt a code of conduct, the workers may be unaware of this. Hence, companies must inform their workers and management of the code of conduct, including translating their codes into local languages. A better approach than simply informing workers is to involve working children and workers' representatives in the drawing up of the code of conduct. This will help companies to understand how children view work and what action child workers want companies to take.

A third concern is enforcement. Unless an adequate enforcement procedure is set in place, then a code is of little value. Enforcement is particularly important because codes of conduct are voluntary. For example, the World Federation of the Sporting Goods Industry (WFSGI) developed a code of conduct for its members in 1997, which was revised in 2000. Included in the code are statements on wages and child labour:[9]

> Employers recognise that wages are essential to meeting employee's basic needs and that employees should be fully compensated for all time worked. In all cases, wages must equal or exceed the minimum wage or the prevailing industry wage, whichever is higher.
>
> No person shall be employed at an age younger than 15 (14 where the law of the country of manufacture allows) or younger than the age for completing compulsory education in the country of manufacture where such age is higher than 15.

The code recognises the need both to provide adults with a decent wage and to protect young children. The problem has been one of implementation. In 2000, the India Committee of the Netherlands (2000) with the cooperation of the South Asia Coalition on Child Servitude (SACCS) published the report 'The Dark Side of Football'. The report claimed that there were still 10 000 children involved in football stitching in the Punjab, India. The report also claims that the wages are generally far below the minimum wage. These claims have been firmly rejected by the Sports Goods Foundation of India and the WFSGI[10] but this case does show the need for independent monitoring of the implementation of companies' codes of conduct. The Global March Against Child Labour launched a new campaign against child labour in football production in May 2001. One of the main objectives of this campaign is for FIFA to set up an independent inspection system, involving trade unions and NGOs, in all the countries that supply sporting goods companies with FIFA-licensed goods.

Establishing effective monitoring systems is essential if the codes of conduct are to be effectively enforced (Boyden *et al.*, 1998, pp. 308).

While this should include independent organisations, such as NGOs and others with specialist knowledge and experience in protecting working children, it must also include trade unions.[11] Mechanisms are also needed to allow workers to complain if they feel that the code is broken, and action taken to remedy any breaches of the code. Finally, in addition to ongoing monitoring of codes of conduct, there is a need for evaluating the long-term impact of codes of conduct on working children and adult workers. Such evaluations are crucial to assess the actual significance of codes of conduct to children's welfare.

Companies have taken measures to end or regulate the employment of children in their factories or in workshops making their products, but less attention has been given to child labour further down in supply chains. This is particularly the case in relation to the extraction or production of raw materials undertaken on small farms or in small-scale industries. This is more difficult to monitor, but NGOs and trade unions have been arguing that companies have an ethical responsibility to ensure that their entire supply chains, from production or extraction of materials through to the manufacture of products, have not involved the exploitation of children. The Ethical Trading Initiative, for example, expects all of its corporate members to agree to and observe international labour standards in their supply chains, including those relating to child labour (Blowfield, 2001).

In relation to the sports industry, how many companies that claim to be free of child labour actually monitor the tanning processes for the leather they use? Tanning is a hazardous process, and in India tanning is one of the 18 industrial processes in which the employment of children is forbidden under India's *Child Labour (Regulation and Prohibition) Act* of 1986 (Human Rights Watch, 1995). Yet research undertaken by Christian Aid in 1997 found children as young as ten working in tanneries producing leather for footballs (Christian Aid, 1997). While sports goods importers have taken action to phase out child labour in football production in Pakistan and elsewhere, there appears to have been less attention given to the employment of children for the more hazardous work in tanneries. The labour conditions in the tanning process of leather used in football production are not, for example, covered in the WFSGI code of conduct.

In relation to agriculture, many international companies do not directly employ producers but purchase commodities produced on small family farms. Monitoring child labour in the production of such commodities is necessary but it is complicated. Children make an important contribution to family farms in most developing countries but, as was discussed above, this becomes harmful to children when the work is hazardous or when the children work such long hours that it interferes with education. While small family farms are exempt from ILO Convention 138, they are covered by ILO Convention 182 on the worst forms of child labour. The challenge for companies is to ensure that their supply chains are not infringing Convention 182.

A good example that illustrates this concerns tobacco production in Brazil. In February 2002, Christian Aid published a report which raised serious concerns about how British American Tobacco (BAT) was abusing its power as a multinational through its Brazilian subsidiary Souza Cruz (Christian Aid, 2000). One of the findings of this report was that many children of farmers participate in tobacco production and are at risk from coming into contact with highly toxic pesticides. Farmers are locked into a contract with Souza Cruz that not only requires the use of these pesticides but also does not pay them enough to employ adult labourers. Many farmers depend on the labour of their own children to make tobacco production economically viable. BAT claims that they are against the employment of children in tobacco production but their current contractual system with small farmers encourages the participation of farmers' children in hazardous forms of work.

Another example concerns the use of child labour in the cocoa industry in the Ivory Coast, which received much media interest in 2001 following revelations of child slavery. Of particular concern were the large numbers of children that were alleged to have been trafficked from Mali and Burkina Faso to work in slave-like conditions on cocoa plantations in the Ivory Coast. Subsequently, chocolate manufacturers have been accused of profiting from child labour and of ignoring the fact that the cocoa that they use has been produced by forced child labour. This is a complicated situation, for which there is inadequate research and information. Cocoa plantations in the Ivory Coast are not large commercial enterprises but small family farms. Children of farmers have always participated in family agriculture, including cocoa production, but many farmers also employ labour migrants from Mali and Burkina Faso, and it is the age and working conditions of these migrant workers that have concerned NGOs in the country. There is a long tradition of labour migration from the Sahelian countries to the Ivory Coast, especially among young men and women. Most are uneducated and work as labourers, domestic workers or in other unskilled jobs, and are easily exploited. A UNICEF report in 1998 estimated that there were 15 000 Malian children working on cocoa plantations in the Ivory coast.

Chocolate manufacturers in Britain have no direct involvement in cocoa production, and the supply chain is more extended than the case of tobacco in Brazil. Farmers sell the raw cocoa to local middlemen who then sell to national intermediaries, who in turn sell to commodity brokers. Chocolate manufacturers then buy from the commodity brokers, and are thus four steps removed from the cocoa farmers. Chocolate manufacturers initially maintained that they were unaware of any forced child labour in cocoa production in the Ivory Coast. However, in response to pressure from NGOs and governments, the industry has agreed to cooperate in an initiative to monitor and investigate the situation.

Conclusion

This chapter has shown that there are no easy solutions to child labour and companies enter a potential minefield when applying corporate social responsibility to the issue. The complexity of child labour in developing countries means that inappropriate action to eliminate child labour, whether by the private sector, the state or civil society, can be potentially harmful to children. Child labour in the export sector cannot be addressed in isolation and must build on the lessons learnt by child-rights organisations over the past decade.

Companies can take concrete steps themselves in developing an ethical approach to child labour. In the long term, an ethical approach to child labour must be centred on providing adults decent wages and conditions of employment; in developing countries, children will continue to work while there are inadequate employment opportunities for adults. This applies not just to company employees but also to those working for subcontractors. It has been argued in this paper that companies engaged in international business have an ethical, if not legal, responsibility to adhere to international labour standards set out in ILO Conventions. In relation to the employment of children, the basic standard that should be enforced in relation to the employment is ILO Convention 138 on the minimum age. In the short term, companies must phase out child labour responsibly but immediate action must be taken to remove children from hazardous types of work, as defined by ILO Convention 182 on the Worst Forms of Child Labour. For children engaged in other types of work, a more gradual approach is needed. This will mean improving working conditions for child labourers and access to good education.

But the scale of the problem means that companies cannot eliminate child labour on their own. One of the central arguments in this paper is that companies, trade unions, NGOs and governmental bodies all play crucial roles (International Labour Organisation, 2001). Government regulation is necessary to establish legally binding requirements on companies in relation to child labour. Law enforcement must be in place to compel recalcitrant companies to comply. Trade union involvement ensures that the interests of the wider labour force are represented through collective bargaining and provides a means of monitoring labour practices. NGOs can provide a strong child-centred perspective, from specialist knowledge about the wider social and economic context of child labour and experience of developing effective means of assisting working children. There are no single mechanisms for bringing these bodies together. In some cases it may be possible to develop partnership agreements; in other cases the relationship may be more one of consultation and dialogue, while in yet others confrontation and conflict may be necessary. Whatever relationship or mechanism is required, the overall objective must be to promote the best interests of children and bring about genuine, long-term improvements in the lives of children.

Notes

1 US Department of Labor, Bureau of International Labor Affairs (1994).
2 Websites of these organisations: The Global March Against Child Labour and SACCS share a common website – *www.globalmarch.org*; the ILO website is *www.ilo.org/childlabour*. Other useful websites are UNICEF *www.unicef.org*, International Save the Children Alliance *www.savethechildren.net*, Anti-Slavery International *www.antislavery.org*, Christian aid *www.christian-aid.org.uk*.
3 Boyden *et al.* (1998), especially chapter 4.
4 *See* Global March Against Child Labour (2000) and NGO Group for the Convention on the Rights of the Child – Sub-group on Child Labour (2001).
5 Save the Children UK, 'Child Labour Project, Sialkot – Programme Description' (n.d.).
6 *Ibid.*
7 Dwight Justice, 'The New Codes of Conduct and Social Partners', International Confederation of Free Trade Unions paper (*www.icftu.org*) (2000).
8 Justice, *op. cit.*
9 WFSGI *Code of Conduct – Guiding Principles* available at *www.wfsgi.org/SGI/activities/Code_Conduct.htm*
10 'Missed Goals', *India Today*, 9 July 2001.
11 Justice, *op. cit.*

References

Anker, R. (2000) 'The economics of child labour: a framework for measurement', *International Labour Review*, vol. 139, no. 3, pp. 257–80.

Anti-slavery International (1996) *Helping Business to Help Stop Child Labour: Comments on How Company Codes of Conduct, 'Child Labour Free' Labels and the Social Clause Can Help Eliminate Child Labour*, London: Anti-Slavery International.

Blowfield, M. (2001) 'Governance and Supply Chains: An Ethical Approach to Responsibility', *Corporate Governance International*, December 2001 (*see also* ETI website *www.ethicaltrade.org*).

Boyden, J., Ling, B. and Myers, W. (1998) *What Works for Working Children*, Florence: UNICEF.

Christian Aid (1994) *Pulling the Rug on Poverty: Child Workers in the Indian Carpet Industry*, London: Christian Aid.

Christian Aid (1997) *A Sporting Chance: Tackling Child Labour in India's Sports Goods Industry*, London: Christian Aid.

Christian Aid (2000) *Hooked on Tobacco: A Report by Christian Aid and DESER on British American Tobacco subsidiary Souza Cruz*, London: Christian Aid. (*see www.christian-aid.org.uk/indepth*).

Global March Against Child Labour (2000) *Ending the Worst Forms of Child Labour: A Guide to Action*, New Delhi: Global March Against Child Labour.

Green, D. (1998) *Hidden Lives: Voices of Children in Latin America and the Caribbean*, London: Save the Children UK and Latin America Bureau.

Human Rights Watch (1995) *The Small Hands of Slavery: Bonded Child Labour in India*, New York: Human Rights Watch.

India Committee of the Netherlands (2000) *The Dark Side of Football: Child and Adult Labour in India's Football Industry and the Role of FIFA*, Utrecht: India Committee of the Netherlands.

International Labour Organisation (2001) *Eliminating the Worst Forms of Child Labour: An Integrated and Time-bound Approach – A Guide for Governments, Employers, Workers, Donors and Other Stakeholders*, Geneva: International Labour Organisation/International Programme on the Elimination of Child Labour.

NGO Group for the Convention on the Rights of the Child – Sub-group on Child Labour (2001) *Brochure on the New ILO Worst Forms of Child Labour Convention*, Geneva: Sub-group on Child Labour.

Ravi, A. (2001) 'Combating Child Labour with Labels: Case of Rugmark', *Economic and Political Weekly*, March 31, pp. 1141–7.

Save the Children (2000a) *Children's Rights: Reality or Rhetoric – The UN Convention on the Rights of Child*, The First Ten Years, London: Save the Children.

Save the Children (2000b) *Big Business, Small Hands: Responsible Approaches to Child Labour*, London: Save the Children.

Thorat, S.K. (1999) 'Poverty, Caste and Child Labour in India: The Plight of Dalit and Adivasi Children', in K. Voll (ed.) *Against Child Labour: Indian and International Dimensions and Strategies*, Berlin Studies in International Politics, New Delhi: Mosaic Books/TMT.

US Department of Labor, Bureau of International Labor Affairs (1994) *By the Sweat and Toil of Children, Vol. 1, The Use of Child Labour in American Imports*, US Dept of Labor: Washington, DC.

Comments by R. Stephen Rubin

I take it that I am replying to Andrew Clayton's chapter, not merely from my own company, Pentland Group, but on behalf of the sports industry and, possibly, industry in general. Pentland is a financial supporter of the Global March Against Child Labour,[1] which has led to the ILO's adoption of Convention 182. We are also proud to have been the initiator of the campaign against the use of children manufacturing footballs in India. Clearly there is a confluence of interests between Andrew Clayton and myself. Any notion that using child labour is in our business interests has to be ridiculous. We believe that the demand for cheap labour by multinational companies refers more to the competitiveness of the country in which goods are manufactured, rather than to specific classes of society within that country. We require a quality product and, if our business in going to exist in 20 years' time, our customers will be in India and China. It is therefore in our interests that these countries develop, which they cannot do on the back of child labour.

No one can argue that child labour is a good thing. We would also agree that we all have some responsibility to do something about it. However, you cannot argue that because NGOs have limited budgets, the private sector must take responsibility for funding. The problem is much more complex and, while poverty is the major factor, if countries themselves cannot tackle it, and NGOs do not have the resources, it is impossible to think of companies doing any thing else but use their best endeavours. Furthermore, if only 5 per cent of child labourers work in the export sector, it is unrealistic to expect multinationals (by their very nature working around the globe) to take on the 95 per cent of the problem for which they cannot bear any responsibility in every country in which they operate. By actually buying products from a country, multinationals are already helping its citizens and not harming them.

There are several areas for discussion arising from Andrew Clayton's chapter.

What can companies reasonably do to tackle child labour in their supply chains?

Where large companies are involved (in our case Nike, Adidas, Reebok and ourselves) there is a capacity (developed over the past few years) to analyse and deal with the issue. (Though even we can get it wrong.) However, most companies in the apparel or sporting goods industry are much smaller and do not have the personnel or the resources to act other than precipitously, and probably inappropriately. This is why Pentland has invested an incredible amount of time and effort to mount collective action in programmes in Pakistan and India on child labour. These partnerships (which include both small companies supplying and small companies buying, together with NGOs, INGOs such as UNICEF and the ILO) take time to set up and inevitably come up with long-term and complex programmes to address the issues. Our role, therefore, becomes one of facilitating the local institutions and the wider civil society to take on the problem and, with our help, improve the situation. We cannot do it on our own; we cannot do it quickly. We have to take account of a wide range of views. We recognise a responsibility but also recognise our limitations.

We must be careful about interfering in the customs of others

In the case of Pakistan, the focus on child labour initially completely blinded us to the fact that more than half the workforce was female, who would not be able to come into the large stitching centres set up through the programme. The entirely laudable desire to create a more formal work relationship without child labour inadvertently marginalised female workers. The result was a severe decrease in the available labour force and loss of income for many families. Subsequently, the programme was changed to take account of that, but the deed had been done. The problem here was the lack of good research, the need to come up with a response quickly because of media attacks (and even that took a year) and the weakness of the local institutions, including government.

Is the media keeping the distinction between child work and child labour?

We can all agree to prioritise actions on child labour where the child is at risk physically, emotionally and mentally, and not attending school. However, both UNICEF and Save the Children have declared that for older children (12–14 years) football stitching is not hazardous. It is, in fact, the best-paying of all the jobs available to young workers who are also attending school. This has been found particularly in Jalandhar (India), where school attendance was far greater than in Sialkot (Pakistan).

Yet because sports sells advertising, the media has concentrated on football stitching, even though this covers less than half-a-per cent of sports industry sales. While not defending child labour in any way, I think it is fair to say that, in Pakistan, earning some money actually assists many children to continue their schooling, since they contribute to the purchase of their school books. Of course, the time that they are spending on the work is crucial. In India, they have decided that up to ten hours per week is about right.

Right of the child to work

Increasingly, we are finding that employers in developing countries are using a minimum age of 18 even though local law and international law allow certain kinds of work from 12–13 years. In the UK, the minimum age for non-hazardous work is 16 and for light work not interfering with education it is 13. We then have the stupidity of children over 14 in India or Bangladesh being unable to work for many export factories. The factories report that this is what their customers 'demand'. We occasionally find under age children in factories, say 13-year-olds, often with false documents. The young person does not see it in their interest to be 'rehabilitated'. In their eyes and those of their family and peers, they are grown up. They don't want to be rehabilitated; they don't want to go back into education. What do we do? What is right for that child?

The International Working group on Child Labour published a paper in 1998, called *Forgotten on the Pyjama Trail*, criticising the action taken by Marks & Spencer after a World in Action programme in 1996 slandering them, when they instructed their supplier, Desmond & Sons, not to employ girls under the age of 15. Rehabilitation programmes for child labour have been notoriously expensive and difficult. Most have been expensive failures because the root causes of the problem have not been addressed. It is a question of balancing resources with a realistic possibility of success for the child or children in question.

Resources and role of Government

In the case of children stitching footballs in India, the Government decided that of all the priorities in child labour (child prostitution, glass industry, *beedi* production, fireworks, brasswear, and so on), devoting resources to a small number of children performing relatively non-hazardous work in one of the richest regions in India was just not on. This attitude applied to the Government and also to many NGOs who would otherwise be willing to work on the issue. The answer was to mobilise the local civil society to garner the resources needed to raise awareness for children to be educated, improve resources in schools and teacher training. This takes a long time. However, in the case of Jalandhar, India, this *has* happened and a wide number of organisations have collectively decided on goals to achieve 100 per cent primary school education within the next few years. This has the added benefit of applying to all sectors in Jalandhar including those factories supplying the domestic market (where much of the problem was and remains) as well as those supplying the export market. A great result, but not one the rest of the world particularly wants to hear.

It is easy to assess age?

Since 2000, Pentland has been working with the International Programme on the Elimination of Child Labour of the International Labour Organisation (ILOfIPEC), Save the Children Fund and UNICEF in Indonesia to see if we can come up with a small pamphlet to be used by personnel officers in factories which would take the following form: clarification of the law and international norms, possible forms of documentation to verify age (ID, school leaving certificate) and medical details by means of non-invasive interview questions. This is not easy as it is extremely difficult to establish what is possible, what is ethically acceptable, who is competent, and so on.

Is it easy to say codes have to be enforced or monitored?

The Ethical Trading Initiative, of which Pentland and Christian Aid are members, is struggling to identify who can do it, how can they do it and who is going to pay for it. Fundamentally, the government of the country where there is child labour has the responsibility to make a standard (the law) and to monitor its adherence. If the labour inspectorates were doing even half a job, then there would be much less of a problem. Ironically, the programme of the ILO to help governments establish and train labour inspectorates and health and safety departments attracts the least funding from member governments.

Surely any programme on child labour must include, for sustainability, the local labour inspectorate in cooperation with the education department. That is how it is done in most countries. At the moment, programmes (Pakistan on footballs, India with carpets and Bangladesh with clothing) have not achieved a balance between the cost of monitoring (very high) and addressing the root causes of the problem. In effect, the programmes are in danger of pushing the problem elsewhere. So far, NGOs and trade unions have not easily fulfilled this role. They do not have the expertise and they do not clearly see their role in doing so. So far the breach has been filled to a certain extent by audit companies such as PriceWaterhouseCoopers and qualification certification agencies such as SGS, ITS and BVQI. These companies are not finding this easy and, apart from anything else, are not finding it easy to make any money from it. They also lack expertise in engaging with civil society to find solutions to problems like child labour. This is simply not what they are good at.

How far does company responsibility go?

Pentland has gone further than most companies in tracking back along the supply chain, especially in the area of home working. We recognised that for many women home working is often their only option to earn money. To insist that all work has to be in the formal setting would be discriminatory and deprive sometimes the poorest people of a living. Research and programmes have been initiated in Portugal, Pakistan, India and China. Tanning, weaving, spinning and dyeing facilities have been inspected in some countries. We know, however, that there are problems of child labour in cotton plantations. Where can it end? What is reasonable? What is not? At Pentland we are relatively good at design, sourcing product and selling it – we are not geared up to be the social reformer of the world but we are trying to do our best in difficult economic times.

For good programmes you need good research. We found that both in India and Pakistan the research by the media and NGOs was not good enough to help us find a way forward. In Pakistan it was not until the 4th independent study (after Raasta Development Consultants, UNICEF and ILO) by Save the Children Fund (Marcus and Husselbee, 1997), that we realised the importance of women in production. Who can draw up terms of reference, who can do it, who can fund it?

Conclusion

It should not be forgotten that, in order for an NGO to raise funding, it must obtain the sympathy of its potential donors. It must, therefore, concentrate on what is wrong, rather than compliment the private sector for what it is endeavouring to do, which is never right.

Note

1   See *http://globalmarch.org/index.html*

References

International Working Group on Child Labour (1998) *Forgotten on the Pyjama Trail – A case study of young garment workers in Méknès (Morocco) dismissed from their jobs following foreign media attention*, Amsterdam: International Working Group on Child Labour.

Marcus, R. and Husselbee, D. (1997) *Stitching Footballs – Voices of Children in Sialkot, Pakistan*, London: Save the Children Fund.

5

Corporate Ethics: The Role of Internal Compliance Programmes under the US Sentencing Guidelines

Michael Goldsmith and Amy Bice Larson

Introduction

This chapter addresses the crucial role of internal compliance programmes in policing corporate conduct. In 1991, the United States Sentencing Commission adopted unprecedented sentencing guidelines that reflected a 'carrot and stick' approach to sentencing corporate criminals (Murphy, 2000). For the first time in American history, these guidelines imposed a strict and determinate sentencing scheme upon corporations violating the law. The guidelines required Federal judges to sentence offenders within penalty ranges determined by the nature of the crime, amount of loss and other pertinent factors. To promote good corporate citizenship, chapter 8 of the guidelines allowed substantial sentencing reductions (potentially amounting to 95 per cent) for companies that had established effective compliance programmes designed to detect and deter criminal activity. Potential sentence reductions spurred American business organisations to implement such compliance programmes; however, implementation soon proved problematic, as the guidelines did not define the elements of an effective programme. Moreover, programmes that did not qualify as 'effective' did not qualify for sentencing reduction.

Since the passage of the corporate sentencing guidelines in 1991, corporate counsel has attempted to identify sources that might shed light on the elements of an effective compliance programme. As this issue has not been the subject of appellate litigation, no body of conventional case law exists to provide the direction that lawyers ordinarily seek in such matters. Fortunately, other sources, which include consent decrees, government-imposed Corporate Integrity Agreements, *nolle prosequi* [not to wish to prosecute] decisions and US Justice Department documents provide guidance. Taken together, these materials suggest what elements the Federal Government considers essential to an effective internal compliance programme.

This chapter summarises the origin and impact of internal compliance programmes under the sentencing guidelines and proposes that the hallmark of 'effective' compliance can be identified by examining sources such as Corporate Integrity Agreements, which identify the elements of internal compliance required by the Federal Government in previous cases. In effect, government-imposed Corporate Integrity Agreements may serve as models of effective compliance programmes.

Origins of the Federal Sentencing Guidelines for organisational defendants[1]

Historically, prosecutors have devoted few resources to corporate crime, focusing instead on deterring and punishing individuals. With Watergate as a catalyst, however, efforts shifted toward preventing organisational crime. The Watergate investigations revealed unreported, illegal campaign contributions to domestic and foreign governments and politicians (Zarin, 2000). Not long after the scandal, Congress passed the *Foreign Corrupt Practices Act* (1978), giving the Securities and Exchange Commission (SEC) power to enforce a prohibition against such corporate bribery payments.

In response to the SEC's grant of power under the 1978 Act, the SEC Enforcement Director encouraged 'internal investigations, disclosure to the Board of Directors, correction through policy and procedure audits, [and] hinted at amnesty with SEC regulators'.[2] When Ronald Reagan took office in 1980, however, the SEC emphasised different priorities, no longer encouraging corporate compliance through self-reporting programmes. The Defense Procurement Scandal of the 1980s, however, again prompted stronger corporate regulation. This scandal, which involved price collusion by defence contract bidders, manipulation of bids to favour certain bidders, and the selling of inside information to potential contractors (Pastor, 1995), produced a significant increase in Federal funding for the military and a new commitment to restore public confidence. To promote high standards of business ethics, a consortium of US industry contractors formed the Defense Industry Initiative, based largely on a code of conduct encouraging voluntary disclosure and other methods of self-regulation.

While changes in the defence industry took shape, Federal criminal law also began to adapt. Motivated by a largely unsuccessful penal system that focused on offender rehabilitation, Congress enacted the

Sentencing Reform Act in 1984. The *Sentencing Reform Act* abolished parole and sought to eliminate unwarranted disparity in Federal sentencing. In conjunction with the passage of the *Sentencing Reform Act*, Congress also created the bipartisan United States Sentencing Commission to provide Federal District Court judges with guidelines for determining sentences for convicted offenders. The commission initially focused only on individual punishment, applying a determinate, structured, sentencing philosophy. After the commission instituted the sentencing guidelines for individual offenders in November 1987, three years of debate and study followed, to promulgate sentencing guidelines for organisational offenders.[3]

Initially, the commission staff advanced a basic law and economics approach to organisational sentencing. Focusing on deterrence, this approach based penalties on the loss caused by the crime and the probability of conviction.[4] The law and economics theory reflected the expectation that companies would spend just enough resources to avoid creating the harm that merits a fine. The Sentencing Commission eventually rejected this approach as unworkable, in part because of the difficulty of calculating the fine by estimating the probability of conviction.[5]

The Department of Justice proposed a different approach to organisational sentencing. Fines based only on the amount of loss caused by the offence could decrease slightly if (1) the offence represented an isolated incident, (2) the organisation had bona fide policies and programmes to minimise offences, and (3) the organisation made a substantial effort to prevent the conduct. This approach reflected compliance programmes like those put into place in the defence industry arena by the Defense Industry Initiative.

Simultaneously to the Department of Justice proposal, the corporate community – soon to be at the receiving end of the new organisational sentencing guidelines – offered its own suggestions. The corporations recommended a 'just punishment' approach which provided that fines would start high, but mitigating factors such as compliance programmes and voluntary disclosure before Government discovery could substantially reduce the penalty. Based on culpability, this approach aimed to punish organisations principally for the organisation's failure as a whole rather than just for individual misconduct.

Relying heavily on the corporations' proposal and partly on the Department of Justice's approach, the Sentencing Commission created Chapter 8 of the Sentencing Guidelines, which accepted the 'just punishment' theory in an effort to ensure that an organisation's punishment corresponded to its degree of blameworthiness. The commission also accepted the concept of offering incentives to deter organisational crime.

The scope of Chapter 8

Chapter 8 of the Sentencing Guidelines defines an organisation as a 'person other than an individual', including a corporation, a partnership, an association, a joint-stock company, a union, a trust, a pension fund, an unincorporated organisation, or a non-profit organisation.[6] The Sentencing Commission designed Chapter 8 as a 'stick' to punish criminal violations by organisations, as well as a 'carrot' to entice organisational compliance.

The 'stick' is a fine predicated on a mathematical formula. First, the base fine is calculated. A base fine essentially reflects the severity of the offence and is the greatest of (1) the fine corresponding to the offence level determined by the Sentencing Guidelines, (2) the 'pecuniary gain to the organization from the offence', or (3) 'the pecuniary loss from the offense caused by the organization, to the extent the loss was caused intentionally, knowingly, or recklessly'. Courts use option (1) when determining whether pecuniary gain or loss is unduly complicated or would prolong the sentencing process.[7] Base fines range from $5000 to $72 500 000.[8]

The 'carrot' used to entice organisational compliance is a culpability score, which may mitigate the base fine by up to 95 per cent. A culpability score may be positive or negative. Five points are automatically assigned to the culpability score, but those points can increase or decrease depending on different factors. The score would increase by five, for example, if high-level officials in a 5000 or more employee organisation 'participated in, condoned, or [were] willfully ignorant of the offense.'[9] A possible three-point subtraction could result, on the other hand, if 'the offense occurred despite an effective programme to prevent and detect violations of law'.[10] The final culpability score corresponds to a table that provides a minimum and maximum multiplier to apply to the base fine in determining the fine range.

A more detailed example illustrates how the base fine and the culpability score work together to determine the fine range. If a corporation commits a level-20 offence, the offence level table in § 8C2.4(d) of the Guidelines sets a $650 000 fine. However, if the offence at issue caused $10 million in pecuniary loss, the court will use the greater amount of $10 million as the base fine. Then, to determine the culpability score, the corporation automatically begins with five points, but an effective compliance programme subtracts three points, and if the corporation accepts responsibility another point is subtracted. The resulting culpability score in that case is one. According to the maximum and minimum multipliers in § 8C2, the maximum multiplier for a one-point culpability score is 0.40, with a minimum multiplier of 0.20. The $10 million base fine multiplied by the maximum and minimum multiplier leaves the court with a substantially reduced fine range between $2 million and $4 million (Wallace, 2000).

The 'carrot' of compliance programmes came with a qualifier provided by the commission – the compliance programme must be 'effective'. The commission did not want to offer a possible 95 per cent fine mitigation for a token compliance programme within an organisation. The text of the Sentencing Guidelines does not address what constitutes an effective compliance programme; instead, the commission addresses the issue in commentary. An effective programme 'means a programme that has been reasonably designed, implemented, and enforced so that it generally will be effective in preventing and detecting criminal conduct'.[11] If a compliance programme fails to detect wrongdoing within the company, a court may consider the company's 'due diligence' and the overall context of its operation to determine whether the programme may still be deemed effective (Goldsmith and King, 1997). As the commission wanted to give organisations some flexibility in establishing their compliance programmes, it did not define due diligence explicitly. Guidelines commentary set forth seven minimum steps to an effective compliance programme:[12]

1. Compliance standards and procedures reasonably capable of reducing the prospect of criminal conduct
2. Oversight by high-level personnel, demonstrating leadership commitment to compliance within the organisation
3. Due care in delegating substantial discretionary authority
4. Effective communications with employees, reaching all levels within the organisation
5. Reasonable steps to achieve compliance, such as monitoring auditing systems and having a system for reporting suspected wrongdoing without fear of reprisal
6. Consistent enforcement of compliance standards, including disciplinary mechanisms
7. Upon detection of violation, take reasonable steps to respond and prevent further similar offences.

These seven steps are general enough to allow individual interpretation. However, flexibility, in turn, may produce paralysis, as generalised minimum standards may be too vague to apply with certainty. To achieve greater certainty, lawyers ordinarily look to the courts for guidance. Surprisingly, however, a dearth of cases address what constitutes an effective compliance programme. Fortunately, the absence of definitive standards and explanatory cases has not left a complete vacuum for corporate counsel. In recent years, various court-imposed Corporate Integrity Agreements have shed some light on what the government deems an effective compliance programme.

Chapter 8 in action

Throughout the 1990s, the government fined various stock brokerage firms and banks hundreds of millions of dollars for a variety of major frauds. For example, Daiwa Bank paid $340 million in criminal fines, and Hoffman LaRoche, Ltd. paid $500 million (Kaplan, 2000). The *New York Law Journal* has observed that the reason for Federal enforcement efforts directed toward organisational crime parallels the explanation given by the notorious bank robber Willie Sutton who, when asked why he robbed banks, replied, '[b]ecause that's where the money is'.[13] Given this climate of heightened enforcement and emphasis on targeting asset-rich organisation violators, organisations must know what constitutes an effective compliance programme.

Judicial interpretations of the organisational guidelines. In *re Caremark International Inc. Derivative Litigation* is perhaps the most significant decision regarding Chapter 8 of the Sentencing Guidelines.[14] Caremark, a health-care business, provided patient care and managed care services.[15] It received most of its revenues from providing 'alternative health-care services' such as growth hormone therapy and haemophilia therapy.[16] In violation of the *Anti-Referral Payments Law*, Caremark paid a physician to 'induce him' to distribute a drug marketed by Caremark.[17] After indictment, shareholders brought a derivative action charging Caremark's directors with a breach of fiduciary duty.[18] Caremark had previously entered guilty pleas for health care fraud and agreed to pay $29 million in criminal fines for mail fraud, $129.9 million in civil claim settlements, $3.5 million for violations of the *Controlled Substances Act*, and a $2 million donation to AIDS research.[19] The court's decision dealt directly with the board of directors' responsibility to ensure that their corporation abides by the law.[20] The court explained, '[t]he Guidelines offer powerful incentives for corporations today to have in place compliance programmes to detect violations of law promptly and to report violations to appropriate public officials when discovered, and to take voluntary remedial efforts'.[21] The court explicitly reiterated Sentencing Guidelines standards, suggesting that an effective compliance programme included a reporting system that provided the board with information sufficient to make informed decisions about the corporation's compliance with the law.[22] Although the court did not find the Caremark board of directors personally liable in this circumstance, *Caremark* suggested that, absent an effective compliance programme, Board members might face individual civil liability for corporate offences. Moreover, subsequent cases agree with the *Caremark* result.[23]

The Ninth Circuit Court of Appeals has also decided an important case involving Chapter 8 of the Sentencing Guidelines. The court announced in *United States v. Eureka Laboratories, Inc.*[24] that, even if the Guidelines' range of fines could bankrupt a company, the court has discretion to impose the maximum fine or sentence at the lower fine range.[25] Though this case does not directly address the minimum standards provided by the Guidelines, it demonstrates their potentially severe effect and how an effective compliance programme may mitigate this possibility.

Some District Court dispositions provide additional assistance in determining what constitutes an effective compliance programme. These decisions detail plea agreements requiring organisations to institute or adjust their programmes.

For example, American Airlines pleaded guilty in 1999 for failing to obey safety regulations regarding the shipment of hazardous materials on passenger planes.[26] In addition to the $8 million fine, the District Court required the airline to publish a full-page apology in a local paper, to commence a court-supervised compliance programme at all airports where American accepts cargo shipments, to hire a new vice-president responsible for compliance with Federal requirements, to strengthen employee training, and to create a hotline to allow employees to make anonymous reports. *United States v. Fine Air Services Inc.*[27] also required a company to establish a compliance programme. The case involved a charge that Fine Air Services obstructed justice by concealing evidence about cargo payloads' weights. As well as four years' probation and a $3.5 million fine, the court ordered Fine Air Services to place a 'Compliance Officer' in senior level management and establish a 'state of the art compliance programme'. The court also required the corporation to submit quarterly reports to the court and to establish a committee within the company to monitor compliance.

These cases give a clearer picture of what courts might consider when determining whether a corporation meets the Guidelines' minimum standards for an effective compliance programme. The decision *not* to prosecute a corporation reveals, perhaps to a greater extent than court decisions, what the government considers to be an effective compliance programme.

Nolle prosequi *decisions based on effective compliance programmes.* Several organisations have avoided prosecution because prosecutors recognised the existence of effective compliance programmes, or because these entities promised to implement such a programme. Prosecutors chose not to bring charges against Chiquita Brand International, for example, because it voluntarily disclosed that its subsidiary had illegally dumped waste into a river in Sioux Falls, South Dakota.[28] The Department of Justice 'praise[d] Chiquita for coming forward and initiating this disclosure'.[29] In its press release, the Government explained: 'The Justice Department has a policy that encourages voluntary disclosures of environmental violations by permitting prosecutors to take various factors, including a company's cooperation, prompt disclosure and correction of the violation, into consideration. Other factors considered under the policy include pervasive non-compliance, knowledge of violations by senior officials and the extent of any environmental compliance programme'.[30]

Potomac Electric Power Company (PEC) also voluntarily disclosed a violation. While investigating a kickback scheme between an employee and a subcontractor, PEC discovered that an employee had illegally discharged ash into a protected wetlands area. Because PEC corrected the violation, cooperated completely with the investigation, and fully disclosed the violation, PEC did not face criminal charges, beyond its $975 000 civil penalty.[31]

Another example is the agreement between the US Attorney's office and the giant accounting firm Coopers & Lybrand. Coopers admitted wrongdoing by a partner in charge of its tax department and other employees for conspiring with Arizona's Governor Fyfe Symington to use inside information in securing a State contract. Federal prosecutors based their decision not to prosecute on Coopers' 'good-faith effort to conduct an internal investigation' and the firm's promise to institute a detailed ethics programme, including company-wide training and the hiring of an independent counsel to oversee compliance.[32]

The agreement reached between the government and Coopers & Lybrand reflects another trend in sentencing organisational defendants. As part of a settlement agreement, government agencies often require an offending organisation to enter into a Corporate Integrity Agreement. Because the Government directs and supervises such agreements, they provide valuable insights into what the Government considers an effective compliance programme.

Corporate Integrity Agreements.   In January of 2001, Bayer Corporation entered into an agreement with the US Department of Health and Human Services (HHS) to settle allegations that Bayer had encouraged inflated Medicaid bills for patients receiving AIDS, cancer or haemophilia treatment.[33] Part of the settlement, a five-year Corporate Integrity Agreement, required Bayer to comply with a detailed system of annual reports and investigations by independent reviewing organisations. Bayer is one of over 250 health-care organisations listed on the HHS website that have entered into Corporate Integrity Agreements or settlement agreements with integrity provisions. HHS currently oversees more than 450 such agreements.[34] According to the HHS, the most comprehensive Corporate Integrity Agreements contain the following seven provisions: '(1) Hire a compliance officer/appoint a compliance committee; (2) develop written standards and policies; (3) implement a comprehensive employee-training programme; (4) audit billings to Federal health-care programmes; (5) establish a confidential disclosure programme; (6) restrict employment of ineligible persons; and (7) submit a variety of reports to the OIG.'[35] Corporate Integrity Agreements may share common elements, but agreements are tailored to the 'conduct at issue' and the capabilities of the organisation.[36] Because many different kinds of organisations enter into Corporate Integrity Agreements, HHS explains that 'the integrity agreements often attempt to accommodate and recognise many of the elements of pre-existing voluntary compliance programmes.'[37] Corporate Integrity Agreements are complex; one of the most recent Corporate Integrity Agreements between HHS and TAP Pharmaceutical Products Inc. covers over fifty pages.[38] The Office of Inspector General (OIG) for HHS provides an Annual Report Content Checklist as a guide to organisations submitting the reports as part of a Corporate Integrity Agreement.[39]

Corporate Integrity Agreements are very strict, but perhaps a severe model of corporate compliance is more helpful than limited court decisions in determining how corporations should interpret the minimum standards proposed by the Sentencing Guidelines. If a corporation errs on the side of safety by basing its compliance programme on such strict settlement imposed Corporate Integrity Agreements, it should easily satisfy minimal guideline requirements for an effective programme.

Other developments and possible future developments

One of the most interesting developments concerning the Organizational Sentencing Guidelines, a 1999 Memorandum from the US Department of Justice (DOJ) to all United States Attorneys, 'provides guidance as to what factors should generally inform a prosecutor in making the decision whether to charge a corporation in a particular case'.[40] Deputy Attorney General Eric Holder circulated the memo, which set forth important compliance factors identified by an *ad hoc* group from the Fraud Section of the Justice Department. Recognising that Federal prosecutors are 'more and more often' facing the decision of whether to prosecute corporate crime, the memo gives Federal prosecutors factors to consider in their charging decision.

Section One of the memo sets forth general principles governing corporate prosecution: 'Corporations should not be treated leniently because of their artificial nature', the memo explains, 'nor should they be subject to harsher treatment'. The memo, however, emphasises that 'first and foremost' government attorneys should recognise that corporate prosecutions can provide unique public benefits: if a corporation is indicted for criminal conduct common to an industry, an indictment can lead to 'deterrence on a massive scale'.

The Holder memo also sets out specific factors prosecutors should consider in deciding whether to indict a corporation, and cites seven factors unique to a 'corporate target':

1. The nature and seriousness of the offence, taking the potential risk to the public into account
2. The pervasiveness of the crime within the corporation, considering the involvement of management as part of this determination
3. The corporation's criminal history of offences, especially offences similar to the offence in question
4. Timely and voluntary disclosure by the organisation of its offence, and its cooperation during investigations
5. The existence of an adequate corporate compliance programme
6. Remedial actions taken by the corporation, including 'efforts to implement an effective compliance programme or to improve an existing one'
7. The consequences to other parties, such as shareholders and innocent employees
8. The alternative remedies beyond criminal prosecution.

Factors 5 and 6 pertain most directly to compliance programmes. In discussing factor 5, Holder acknowledges that 'the Department has no formal guidelines for corporate compliance programmes'.[41] Prosecutors should ask two fundamental questions, however, when assessing the effectiveness of a compliance programme: 'Is the corporation's compliance programme well designed?'[42] and 'Does the corporation's compliance programme work?'[43] Essentially, the prosecutor must determine if the compliance programme is merely a 'paper programme', or whether it is effective. More specific guidance comes in Holder's explanation that the compliance programmes should target detection of those crimes most likely to typify a corporation's particular type or business.

After an offence is discovered or disclosed, factor 6 requires corporations to convince prosecutors that 'the corporation's focus is on the integrity and credibility of its remedial and disciplinary measures rather than on the protection of the wrongdoers'.[44] Prosecutors should look for signs of internal discipline. Compliance programmes and changes made to improve existing compliance programmes are indicative of internal discipline.[45]

While the specifics of the Holder memorandum may help identify elements of an effective compliance programme, its mere existence and nationwide distribution are perhaps of greater significance. The government thereby sent a strong message to corporations that the Department of Justice is serious about targeting and prosecuting organisational offenders. Additionally, the memo reiterated the government's endorsement of the 'carrot and stick' approach contained in the Sentencing Guidelines.

Adopting compliance programmes, however, is not without risk. Compliance programmes have produced an unanticipated dilemma for many businesses: when a company responds to the Sentencing Guidelines by starting a comprehensive compliance programme aimed at promoting lawful conduct, it risks generating incriminating information that may increase the risk of criminal or civil liability.[46] For example, to qualify for mitigation under the Sentencing Guidelines, responsible corporations must institute programmes to assess their compliance with applicable laws and to prevent illegal conduct within the workplace[47] (Gruner, 1994). These compliance programmes and audits inevitably generate a variety of information and materials ranging from objective facts and photographs to subjective evaluations, reports and opinions.[48] Under present law, compliance programme and audit materials are rarely confidential. Consequently, they may be subject to disclosure both in criminal investigations and during civil actions against the company.[49] Unless protected, these materials threaten to become a litigation road map for prosecutors and private plaintiffs (Allen and Hazelwood, 1987).

Since the institution of the Organizational Sentencing Guidelines, judicial and legislative attempts to protect materials generated in administering compliance programmes have been sporadic.[50] Without legal protections, companies are in the difficult position of choosing between deciding which risk is greater: not creating a compliance programme and forfeiting any chance of mitigating fines; or establishing a corporate compliance programme that may generate incriminating evidence. The 'carrot' of an effective compliance programme becomes less attractive when compliance materials are not protected.[51] Although the work product doctrine, attorney–client privilege, various statutes, and some common-law evidentiary privileges may protect compliance materials in some circumstances, 'these protections are narrowly drawn and lack certainty'.[52] Immunity for compliance materials may solve this quandary posed by the Sentencing Guidelines. Thus far, no courts have addressed this issue.

Conclusion

After only a decade of existence, the 'carrot and stick' approach advanced by the Sentencing Guidelines is no longer controversial. Compliance programmes have become an accepted and crucial part of most major US corporations. As policing corporate crime is likely to remain a prosecutive priority, organisations interested in avoiding indictment – or at least, significantly reducing criminal sanctions – must continue their efforts to define and implement effective compliance programmes.

Notes

1   This section relies heavily on Desio (2001).
2   *See* Desio, *supra* note 2, p. 27.
3   Nagel and Swenson (1993).
4   *Ibid.*, p. 219 (quoting *United States Sentencing Commission, Preliminary Draft Sentencing Guidelines* (September 1986)).
5   *Ibid.*
6   United States Sentencing Guidelines (USSG), § 8A1.1 (2001).
7   *Ibid.* § 8C24.c.
8   *Ibid.* § 8C24.d.
9   *Ibid.* § 8C2.5b(1)(A)(i).
10   *Ibid.* § 8C2.5(f).
11   USSG, § 8A1.2 cmt. (3(k))
12   USSG, § 8A1.2 cmt. (3(k (1–7)).
13   Francis J. Serbaroli, 'Feds Targeting Big Pharmaceutical Companies', *New York Law Journal*, 30 March 2001.
14   698 A.2d 959 (Del. Ch. 1996).
15   *Ibid.*, p. 960.
16   *Ibid.*
17   *Ibid.*, p. 962.
18   *Ibid.*, p. 964.
19   *Ibid.*, p. 965 n. 10.

20 *Ibid.*, pp. 967–72.
21 *Ibid.*
22 *Ibid.*
23 *See In re* W.R. Grace & Co., 65 SEC Docket 1240, 1997 WL 597984 (30 September 1997); *McCall v. Scott*, (M.D. Tex 1997).
24 103 F.3d 908 (9th Cir. 1996).
25 *Ibid.*, p. 912.
26 United States v. American Airlines, Inc., Case No. 99–00902-CR (S.D. Fla. 16 December 1999).
27 Case No. 00-221-CR-LENARD-02 (S.D. Fla. 30 June 2000).
28 Dept of Justice News Release, 21 February 1996 or 1996 WL 72865 (D.O.J.).
29 Dept of Justice News Release, 7 February 1996, *available at http://www.usdoj.gov/opa/pr/1996/February 96/035.txt*
30 *Ibid.*
31 Kate Shatzin, 'Potomac Electric Pays Fine to Settle Fly Ash Violation', *Baltimore Sun*, 4 July 1995, B3.
32 *See* Andy Pastor, 'Coopers Settles in Symington Dealings', *Wall Street Journal*, 23 September 1996, B12.
33 *Ibid.*
34 United States Department of Health and Human Services, Office of Inspector General, *available at http://oig.hhs.gov/fraud/cia/index.html*
35 *Ibid. available at http://oig.hhs.gov/fraud/cias.html*
36 *Ibid.*
37 *Ibid.*
38 *Ibid. available at http://oig.hhs.gov/fraud/cia/agreements/tap_pharmaceutical_products_ 92801.pdf*
39 *Ibid. available at http://oig.hhs.gov/cia/ciachecklist.htm*
40 Memorandum from Deputy Attorney General Eric Holder, to all Component Heads and United States Attorneys, 'Bringing Criminal Charges Against Corporations' (16 June 1999), at *http://www.usdoj.gov/criminal/fraud/policy/Chargingcorps.html*
41 *Ibid.*
42 *Ibid.*
43 *Ibid.*
44 *Ibid.*
45 *Ibid.*
46 This discussion relies heavily on Goldsmith and King (1997).
47 *See* Gruner (1994, § 8.3–8.3.3).
48 *See* Valukas *et al.* (1993–1995, § 5:03, pp. 2–4).
49 Brown and Kandel (1990, 2–19 to 2–35).
50 Goldsmith, *supra* note 15, p. 39.
51 *Ibid.*, p. 41.
52 *Ibid.*, p. 22.

References

Allen, R.J. and Hazelwood, C.M. (1987) 'Preserving the Confidentiality of Internal Corporate Investigations', *Journal of Corporation Law*, vol. 12, no. 2, pp. 355–81.

Brown, L.M. and Kandel, A.O. (1990) *The Legal Audit*, New York: Clark Boardman Callaghan.

Desio, P. (2001) *Fundamentals of Organizational Compliance*, New York: Practising Law Institute.

Goldsmith, M. and King, C.W. (1997) 'Policing Corporate Crime: The Dilemma of Internal Compliance Programs', *Vanderbilt Law Review*, vol. 50, p. 1.

Gruner, R.S. (1994) *Corporate Crime and Sentencing*, Charlottesville, VA: Michie.

Kaplan, J.M. (2000) 'Justice's Guidance on Prosecuting Corporations: A 'Booster Shot' for Ethics Officers', *Ethikos and Corporate Conduct Quarterly*, July/August 2000, vol. 14, no. 1.

Murphy, J.E. (2000) *Evaluations, Incentives and Rewards in Compliance Programs: Bringing the Carrot Indoors*, New York: Practising Law Institute.

Nagel, I.H. and Swenson, W.M. (1993) 'The Federal Sentencing Guidelines for Corporations: Their Development, Theoretical Underpinnings, and Some Thoughts About Their Future', *Washington University Law Quarterly*, vol. 71, p. 205.

Pastor, A. (1995) *When the Pentagon Was For Sale: Inside America's Biggest Defense Scandal*, New York: Scribner.

Valukas, A.R., Stauffer, R.R. and Murphy, J.E. (1993–95) *Threshold Considerations*, in J.M. Kaplan, J.E. Murphy and W.M. Swenson (eds) *Compliance Programs and the Corporate Sentencing Guidelines: Preventing Criminal and Civil Liability*, New York: Clark Boardman Callaghan.

Wallace, G.J. (2000) *Introduction to the Organizational Sentencing Guidelines*, New York: Practising Law Institute.

Zarin, D. (2000) *Doing Business Under the Foreign Corrupt Practices Act*, New York: Practising Law Institute.

Comments by Simon Deakin

This is an important chapter for the UK debate on how to ensure compliance with ethical norms through regulatory legislation and shareholder pressure. The chapter has much to tell us about the US experience.

Firstly, in the US there is an extensive body of legislative regulation at both Federal and State level – 'hard law' in the areas of competition law, anti-trust, bribery and corruption, economic crime, environmental protection and occupational health and safety.

Secondly, as the paper explains, there are powerful incentives for companies to put into place internal compliance systems, partly because of the very powerful stick, which arises out of the possibility of what are – by UK standards – enormous fines being levied against companies. There is also the possibility that individual company officers may face criminal sanctions of certain kinds under circumstances which would rarely arise in the UK.

Thirdly, an important feature of the US system, which the case law discussed in the paper illustrates, is that shareholder pressure may be exercised through civil proceedings, or what is known as the shareholders' 'derivative action'. The legal system enables shareholders to sue individual directors and the board collectively if there has been a major breach of a fiduciary duty or a breach of the duty of care owed by directors to the company (and, in effect, to the shareholders). This means that if a board permits a serious breach of the criminal law to take place by virtue of the company's activities, the directors may find themselves individually responsible for the consequences, again producing powerful incentives.

Fourthly, the notion of organisational responsibility is a major part of the relevant US law. That is another major point of difference with the UK experience. In the UK, although it is of course possible for corporations to commit crimes, there is reluctance to allow corporate liability to arise in a criminal context in cases where no individual manager or director can also be held personally responsible. We see that most clearly in the long-running debate about whether to institute a new offence of corporate manslaughter as well as the difficulty in bringing criminal charges against managers and directors arising out of catastrophic accidents (Ridley and Dunford, 1997). Very often, we find that the individual employee – the driver in a train crash, for example – ends up shouldering the blame in the sense of being the only party to be subject to a criminal prosecution. The organisational or managerial failure, which may have made the individual's job difficult in the first place, is not addressed adequately by the criminal law system.

In addition, shareholder pressure cannot be exercised against boards in the UK as it can in the US because the UK civil procedure system does not hold out the same possibility of derivative suits being brought. Also, large damages awards against boards of the kind that are observed from time to time in the US context are not observed in the UK.

The chapter also highlights the role of market forces operating via reputational effects. The harm done to a company's reputation by legal action is factored into the share price of that company. Those companies which upset public opinion trade at a discount to the market; but that presupposes legal action against them. Litigation brings to the public's attention the failure of companies to comply with generally accepted standards.

There are lessons for the UK which I will consider very briefly. If we were to go down the US path, we would have to contemplate extending organisational corporate responsibilities and liabilities for breach of legislative regulations, and not tolerating a situation in which the blame is simply shifted onto individual employees without managerial responsibilities. In addition, we would need to improve the internal auditing and reporting systems of companies, so that boards clearly have the responsibility of ensuring that there are adequate internal reporting mechanisms and information flows coming up from the employees to the managers and thence to board level. That agenda is set out in the Turnbull report (ICEAW, 1999), which has the potential to be an important turning point in the UK debate. It makes it clear that a major failure in the area of health and safety regulation, or a similar form of regulation, has implications for shareholder value and not just for the other stakeholders such as customers and employees. The dramatic collapse of the share price of Railtrack following the Hatfield rail crash in October 2000 and the highly critical Health and Safety Executive Report which was published shortly after (HSE, 2001) is a stark indication of how a major failure of this kind can destroy shareholder value, but this would not have occurred without the presence of external health and safety controls. From a corporate governance viewpoint, the question is why the shareholders were unable to act in advance to protect their interests and, indirectly, those of Railtrack's employees and the travelling public. Shareholders must take more seriously their own role in curbing irresponsible corporate behaviour. There are now signs that they may be willing to do so (Deakin, 2002). An amendment to pensions regulations made in 1999, that came into effect in 2001 requires pension funds to indicate in their statement of investment practices their voting policy and to state their position in relation to social, ethical and environmental investment matters.[1] This has greatly enhanced the importance of ethical investment issues.

Questions that were previously thought to lie in the political sphere alone are now increasingly viewed as relevant to corporate governance. A quiet revolution may just be beginning.

Note

1 The Occupational Pension Schemes (Investment and Assignment, Forfeiture, Bankruptcy, etc.) Amendment Regulations, SI 1999/1849, reg. 2(4), amending SI 1996/3127.

References

Deakin, S. (2002) 'Squaring the circle? Shareholder value and corporate social responsibility in the UK', *George Washington University Law Review*, discussing L. Mitchell, *Corporate Irresponsibility: America's Newest Export*, New Haven, CT: Yale University Press, 2001.

HSE (Health and Safety Executive) (2001) *Train Derailment at Hatfield, Second Interim Report*, 23 January 2001, London: HSE, available at: *http://www. hse.gov.uk/railway/hatfield/interim2.htm*.

ICEAW (Institute of Chartered Accountants of England and Wales) (1999) *Internal Control: Guidance for Directors on the Combined Code*, London: ICAEW.

Ridley, A. and L. Dunford (1997) 'Corporate killing: legislating for unlawful death?', *Industrial Law Journal*, vol. 26, pp. 99–113.

6
The OECD's Anti-bribery Convention

Graham Rodmell

The consequences of international corruption

Corruption is immensely damaging and costly, particularly in the field of North–South development, where the true victims are the poorest and most vulnerable. Uneconomic or unnecessary projects are undertaken which create demands on scarce foreign exchange while the bribes are paid off shore and never enter the host country. Capital contracts cost more than they should, by perhaps 15–20 per cent. Tax revenue is lost. Poorly qualified officials are appointed to senior posts and there is a general lowering of standards in government. Corruption can contribute materially to the collapse of economies and the downfall of political regimes. Surveys have shown that the biggest single deterrent to inward direct investment in a country is the perceived level of corruption.[1]

Corruption results in the misuse of a company's capital, which is invested for corporate purposes. If it is known within a company that its foreign subsidiaries or joint ventures routinely win business by paying bribes, the corporate culture of that company is tarnished.

Corruption distorts markets and is, therefore, the enemy of fair competition. The ease with which the proceeds of corruption can be laundered fuels extortion and has the potential to damage banking reputation and financial markets.

Change in the regulatory environment – the OECD convention

Among the many international initiatives against bribery in business, the 1997 OECD Convention is the most important. All 29 OECD countries and 5 non-member countries signed it. By the end of 2001, only Ireland had failed to ratify it. The convention came into force on 15 February

1999. It is not a perfect instrument, but it is already fundamentally changing the attitude of business and governments.

The convention tackles the 'supply side' of international corruption. Each signatory is required to make it a criminal offence for any person to offer, promise or give any undue pecuniary or other advantage, whether directly or indirectly or through intermediaries, to a foreign public official (widely defined), in order to obtain or retain business or other improper advantage in the conduct of international business. Note that the foreign official can be an official of any state in the world. The convention contains several important provisions designed to make it effective.

The convention had its origins in the US *Foreign Corrupt Practices Act* of 1978, enacted following the Lockheed scandal. In 1975, the US Senate Banking Committee began an investigation into 'questionable' payments made by Lockheed Martin and found that they had paid hundreds of millions of dollars through consultants to government officials in Saudi Arabia, Japan, Italy and the Netherlands in return for aircraft contracts. Bribe recipients included the Prime Minister and Transport Minister in Japan and a $1 m bribe to Prince Bernhard of The Netherlands. The Banking Committee found that while nine different US laws had been criminally violated by a bribe paid abroad, these statutes were only peripherally violated and no specific law explicitly prohibited an American from paying a bribe overseas (Martin, 1999). The *Foreign Corrupt Practices Act* changed that. However, from then on, US business people considered that they were disadvantaged by being penalised while those in other States were free to bribe internationally. Constant US pressure on the major trading states finally resulted in recommendations being adopted by the OECD Council in 1994 and 1996. These related in particular to the modalities and international instruments to facilitate criminalisation of bribery of foreign public officials; tax deductibility of bribes to foreign public officials; accounting requirements, external audit and internal company controls; and rules and regulations on public procurement which led rapidly to signing of the Convention in 1997.[2] Whether or not the convention will be effective in practice will depend on what each exporting country provides in its laws and what measures are taken to enforce the laws.

Areas not covered by the OECD convention

In the interests of achieving a signed convention, some subjects were left unresolved. It does not criminalise bribe payments to foreign political parties or party officials. These offer an obvious way around the criminal offence. Some of the major recorded cases of bribe payments to secure contracts have been made precisely in this way. The Convention is also unclear regarding bribes paid by foreign subsidiary or associated companies.

Impact of the Convention on UK domestic law

Until there is legislation in the UK, the OECD Convention has no direct impact on UK law, which remains as it was. Until there is in our law a clear offence of bribing foreign public officials, bribes to officials negotiated and paid wholly offshore cannot be prosecuted in the UK and remain deductible for tax purposes. In June 2000, the OECD asked the UK Government to enact the necessary laws as a matter of urgency. It was particularly disappointing that the UK, a leading G7 nation, was at that time seen as one of the few laggards.

Present UK law is to be found in the *Prevention of Corruption Acts* of 1889, 1906 and 1916. In addition, there are a variety of obscure and overlapping common law offences. When the OECD convention was being negotiated and signed, our domestic law of corruption was already being reviewed in detail by the Law Commission. Their report, published in March 1998 (Law Commission 1998), recommended that the common law offences should be abolished and that there should be a modern statutory offence.

The Law Commission Report was passed to an interdepartmental Working Group, led by the Home Office, which published a paper in June 2000 (Home Office 2000), setting out the government's proposals for the reform of the domestic law of corruption and for creating the foreign bribery offence required by the international conventions. Unusually, there was to be nationality based extra-territorial jurisdiction for this offence. Following the UK's 2001 general election, the Queen's Speech included measures against corruption. The government proposed to introduce a *Criminal Justice Bill* in January 2002 that would have dealt, among other major law reform proposals, with the law of corruption.

September 11

Following the tragic events of 11 September, the Government decided to enact some fast-track anti-terrorism legislation and decided to drop the proposed *Criminal Justice Bill*. Transparency International (UK) took steps to emphasise the close linkages between corruption, money laundering, organised crime and terrorism. The UK government decided to include in the *Anti-terrorism Bill* (now the *Anti-terrorism, Crime and Security Act* 2001), the provisions necessary to comply with the OECD Convention. Part 12 came into force on 14 February 2002. It takes all the existing domestic offences and enacts that it is immaterial if the relevant actions or functions of the public officials or authorities are carried out in a country outside the UK. Moreover, nationality-based extra-territorial jurisdiction will apply, so that a British national or a UK company may be prosecuted for bribing a foreign public official, even if every part of the offence takes place abroad. The new legislation will apply also to wholly private sector bribery. Moreover, foreign bribes or commissions will cease to be deductible for tax purposes.

Anyone now found guilty of bribing foreign officials could be imprisoned and heavily fined. Many companies operating globally will already have encountered the OECD offence, much as any UK company with a NYSE quote or a US division will have had to comply with the *Foreign Corrupt Practices Act* of the USA.

Regulation and voluntary action – the changing business environment

Concepts of corporate governance are rapidly developing. The rules governing listed companies in the UK require compliance with the Turnbull guidance (ICEAW, 1999). Internal controls have to be adequate to support a company's effective and efficient operation and to enable it to respond to significant business, operational, financial, compliance and other risks. These risks include reputation and business probity issues. Reputation can be damaged by allegations of bribery in another country and by the conduct of a subsidiary, associated or joint venture company.

My impression is that there is at present very little awareness of the new convention in boardrooms or even government departments, embassies and high commissions. This is not surprising. There has been no official information campaign. Some still think that paying commissions is the way 'business is done'. The Foreign Office website on 'Global Citizenship'[3] (April 2002) encourages companies operating abroad to resist corrupt practices and to promote transparency in business activities. It does mention the OECD Convention and the need to comply with the law, but emphasises positive aspects of compliance, including enhanced prospects for economic development and safeguarding corporate reputation and staff morale.

The international climate is changing fast. The convention is affecting attitudes worldwide to corruption in trade and investment. Progressive companies realise that sustainable and profitable international business depends on fair and open competition based on legitimate factors, such as price, terms, specification, quality and delivery, rather than the size of a bribe. Given the movement towards ethical business and investment, (the 'FTSE4Good' index and ethical funds) and the present ease of flow of information around the world, companies operating internationally will not escape the consequences of engaging in corrupt activities.

Articulate groups within civil society can indirectly damage businesses that engage in bribery and corruption, in much the same way as they have those companies accused of exploiting child labour, or destroying the environment or damaging health. Reputation is now seen as a company's single most important asset.

Meeting the challenge

Companies operating in corrupt environments are rightly seen as 'victims', but if they choose to comply with extortion demands, their businesses will be compromised. Managers will assume that payments have to be made to strategically placed individuals, companies or parties. Prices then have to be set to safeguard net profit on the deals and accounts have to be maintained to disguise the real purpose of the payments. 'Backhanders' and facilitation payments become the norm. From being victims, the companies are now part of the corrupt system and actively promoting its growth.

The better approach is to welcome the new legislation. It is good news for companies with excellent products and services. In the short term, some will suffer disadvantages, but those companies looking to remain competitive and to enhance shareholder value into the future will see corrupt business as a serious threat and positive measures to combat it as opportunities. This approach accords with the voluntary OECD Guidelines for Multinational Enterprises which now have a separate chapter on combating bribery.[4]

Business principles for countering bribery

Transparency International, in association with Social Accountability International and a group of private sector interests with experience in many parts of the world, is leading the development of a set of business principles to enable enterprises to combat bribery in all their activities.

The business principles are not intended to comprise a formal 'standard'. Rather, they are designed for use by small, medium and large enterprises and require each enterprise to develop its own programme reflecting its size, business sector and locations of operation. The programme has to be consistent with all relevant laws and should be developed in consultation with employees. It should concentrate on those forms of bribery that pose the greatest risks.

As a minimum, the programme prohibits bribes and kickbacks and provides guidelines for political and philanthropic contributions and the offer or receipt of gifts and hospitality. The policy should make it clear that no employee will suffer demotion or penalty for not paying bribes, even when the enterprise may lose business as a result.

Internal control systems and audit procedures have to support continuous improvement to minimise the risk of bribery and eliminate off-the-books accounts.

An enterprise should ensure that subsidiary companies and joint ventures it controls should adopt the principles and comply with the programme. When an enterprise engages in a new joint venture, it should use its influence to persuade other partners to adopt the principles.

An enterprise should not channel improper payments through an agent and should ensure that:

- agents conform to the requirements of its programme
- agents are hired only for bona fide business purposes
- compensation paid to agents is appropriate and justifiable remuneration for services rendered.

The ICC booklet *Fighting Bribery – a corporate practices manual* (ICC, 2001) lists a number of red flags, which alert companies to possible illicit activities by agents and sales representatives.

Conclusion

Both the criminal law and action by progressive companies are contributing to putting corruption firmly on the list of ethical business concerns. Until now in the UK, responsible business has been well ahead of government and it will probably remain ahead. Criminal sanctions effectively reinforce best business practice. The difference now is that company advisors can no longer even contemplate bribery in order to win business.

Notes

1 *See* Commonwealth Business Council (1999) and Wei (2000).
2 The text of the Convention can be found on the OECD website at: *http://www.oecd.org/EN/document/0,,EN-document-88-nodirectorate-no-6-7198-31,00.html*
3 Under *http://www.fco.gov.uk/news/keythemepage.asp?PageId = 298*
4 The Guidelines can be found on the OECD website at: *http://www.oecd.org/EN/about/0,,EN-about-93-nodirectorate-no-no-no-7,00.html.* Chapter VI of the Guidelines adopted on 27 June 2000 is on combating bribery.

References

Commonwealth Business Council (1999) *Priorities for Action to Promote Investment in the Commonwealth,* Toronto: Commonwealth Business Council.

Home Office (2000) *Raising standards and upholding integrity: the Government's proposals for the reform of the criminal law of corruption in England and Wales,* London: H.M.S.O.

ICC (International Chamber of Commerce) (2001) *Fighting Bribery – A corporate practices manual,* Paris: International Chamber of Commerce.

ICEAW (Institute of Chartered Accountants of England and Wales) (1999) *Internal Control: Guidance for Directors on the Combined Code,* London: ICAEW.

Law Commission (1998) Legislating the Criminal Code: corruption: item 11 of the Sixth Programme of Law Reform: Criminal Law, LAW COM/Law Commission; no. 248, London: HMSO.

Martin, A.T. (1999) 'The Development of International Bribery Law', *Natural Resources and Environment,* Fall, vol. 14, issue 2.

Wei, Shang Jin (2000) 'Local Corruption and Global Capital Flows', *Brookings Papers on Economic Activity,* 2000 issue 2, pp. 303–54.

Comments by Rodney Whittaker

There is no denying that there is a fair amount of humour connected with the topic of bribery and corruption. It is, after all, a topic which everyone understands.

Certainly, when I am doing training sessions on the subject of bribery and corruption around GlaxoSmithKline (GSK), I often start off with a cartoon where there is a group of worthy businessmen with briefcases, who are standing in front of a desk. And behind the desk is the chief of police. A large, very well fed man, he is very content with life, he is not particularly well shaven, and he is saying, 'Of course I can help you gentlemen root out corruption, if you make it worth my while.'

Unfortunately, the cartoon reflects the reality that there are a number of countries in the world where corruption is endemic in all levels of society. What is more, when people say 'There is a law against it', I wonder whether that makes it better or worse, because in virtually all of these countries, there are laws against corruption of public servants and government employees, yet everyone knows that there is corruption happening and the law is being openly flouted every day.

I wanted to say something about what we do about this in GSK. But first, I was interested to hear about Michael Goldsmith's reflections on the US Federal Sentencing Guidelines, and we have seen something of this in action in our US company. I have to say it has been great for the economy, there didn't used to be this huge body of compliance officers, and now there are dozens of them with representatives in every big company. They have a Compliance Officers' Association, a union and they have conventions around the country, which is very good for the hotel industry. It's a whole new area of employment.

And going on in a slightly cynical vein, I can say it has been good for the paper manufacturers. As the lawyers in America will tell you, if it hasn't been documented it hasn't been done. And they're right, you've got to have your paper – and the amount of paper generated in the course of a compliance programme can be formidable.

There is a serious point here: I think it is true of all compliance programmes that, on the one hand, there is the process and the paper; and on the other hand, there is the reality of it. How do you really get your message to 'live' in the organisation? First, I think that it helps if the compliance programme is based on some values, and the company has communicated those values. The compliance programme then does not appear as an isolated event, but something that is related to a bigger picture.

Second, I think you have to realise that the chain is as strong as its weakest link, and this is really quite a long chain both in organisational and geographical terms, stretching from the Chief Executive in the UK or USA and going right down to the sales manager and his sales representatives in (say) South East Asia. In GSK, we had from Day One a booklet on integrity, with the corporate logo, which is signed by the Chief Executive, and that is necessary – he has put his personal stamp on this. But you have to take that down layer by layer in the organisation. For example, the head of the GSK International business, for whom I work, said very deliberately at a meeting of his top-line and staff people words to the effect 'International is going to be clean. We do not want business that comes from bribery. We do not need it, and I do not want it. If I find out it is going on, in any of your areas, you are going to be out of a job.'

He then required all those people to take that message down to the level of their own organisations so they went back to Singapore, to Beijing, to Rio and so on and passed on the same message to their direct reports. There is nothing like the line chief, their boss, looking them in the eye and saying to them, 'Listen to this. I mean this. In my business, I do not want corruption, and if I find that, then you are going to be dismissed.' And that is then to be repeated down at the individual country level.

Now, if you are getting that done, you are making a start. Most of the people who face these issues in their jobs are from the line organisation, not from the headquarters staff. It is the line people who have to make the sales and the profit numbers. And every month, within three of four working days of the end of every month, the figures from their area are going to be faxed up to the top. And they are the people who, if you get it into their heads, then you are really getting somewhere. And that is what you have to do to make these matters 'live' in a big company.

Now you have to inject some humour and involve people because in the training sessions that we do, there is nothing like having a lawyer stand up after lunch and give a lecture to make people go to sleep. This is certainly the case for sales and marketing people, who will question whether it affects their end-of-the-month figures, and draw their own conclusions. So, we always use interactive training. It is not a lecture, because we have already sent out the relevant policies for reading before the meeting.

So we start straight away by putting up on screen a realistic example of potentially corrupt behaviour which relates to the pharmaceutical industry in their country. It may be getting the goods through Customs, it may be some inappropriate promotion of pharmaceutical products, perhaps in hospitals, or whatever, and we say 'This has landed on your desk. You are the manager; would you sign off on this?' And you try to get a discussion going, and you get them involved, considering a realistic everyday project. If you can get them to engage in this, it is something that they can learn from and get some idea of the principles involved.

I think that there's some element of stick and carrot in this. The stick is certainly that if you are a manager, and something happens in your office through corruption or other behaviour, you are going to be held accountable. It is not sufficient simply that you are not corrupt yourself. And we have had instances of this, where we have said to managers 'Look, this is going on in your organisation, we think you should know about it. You are going to lose your job because the organisation for which you were responsible has fouled up in this way.' And we make them aware of that standard to which they will be held.

In terms of the carrot, we are very good at rewarding managers' performance, but how do you reward integrity? How do you reward and recognise people who are taking the right decisions in difficult circumstances? We are always looking for new ideas on how to do that.

Finally, I'd like to mention the new UK law on bribery. We are mainly a US–UK based organisation and for a long time at training sessions I have been able to say 'hands up the US citizens', of whom there are probably a few, and be able to say 'you had better listen carefully, because if you get this wrong you will go to prison as well'. The new UK law will help, because it will increase my vulnerable audience.

So the key question is how you get that message across and get managers to believe it? And that is something that the UK law will help people with in the future, by bringing the subject to people's attention.

7

The Role of Global Institutional Investors – Shareholder Engagement Opportunities for a New Era

Peter Butler

The duty to intervene

I wish to discuss the duty of shareholders to intervene in the companies in which they invest, and how shareholders can create value in doing so. And it is because I believe in this shareholder engagement that I disagree with the view, raised by Simon Deakin earlier in this volume, that it is inevitable that the UK will move towards the US litigation model. Such a view overlooks the fact that shareholders in the UK have many more rights than shareholders in the United States. It is true that shareholders do not always use those rights, but if they are used properly, I think US-style litigation is not necessary.

I will try to explain how international shareholders are learning to work together to harvest the benefits of proactive engagement.

But first, let me introduce myself; I am not actually a fund manager, I have 20 years' commercial and industrial experience including seven years as an executive director. But now I represent one of the largest pension fund managers in Europe, which is Hermes Pensions Management Limited, and my job is to direct our corporate governance programmes, and our shareholder intervention programmes in 3000 public companies worldwide. I would like to say a little more about Hermes because it helps to explain why we are able to play a leading governance role in the UK. Hermes is the executive arm of the BT Pension Scheme, the UK's largest pension fund, and in total we have something like £48 bn under management. Of great significance is that the largest part of our equity holdings are in indices in the UK, the US, Europe and Asia Pacific, and in the UK the weight of money is such that our clients, through Hermes, own over 1 per cent of all the companies in the FTSE All Share Index.

Over the past three years, we have developed the concept of investing in underperforming companies in our Focus Funds, through which we now invest about £600 m. Hermes Focus Funds invest in quoted companies that are underperforming their peers in the same sector. They are stocks that have lost momentum, and that the market as a whole is shunning. We employ shareholder engagement techniques to turn those companies around and help make them more valuable. Hermes is a long-term investor because of our clients' index holdings, and also independent, in that we have no conflicts of interest as do so many other fund managers.

Just to give you an example, most fund managers that you can think of will be owned by banks, or publicly quoted insurance companies. And think of the conflicts for the people that are in the asset management arm, when they have a stock that is performing poorly; they have two choices. They can just sell, which is what active managers usually do, and pass the problem on to somebody else, or they can engage, perhaps with the chief executive of the company in which they are investing, and have some conversations about what should be done to improve performance. If the chief executive does not like the intervention of the fund managers, and he is also a client of the parent bank – he may contact the fund manager's superiors. And of course, what happens is that – well, with human nature as it is – what does the fund manager do? He just sells. Hermes doesn't have any of those conflicts. We are also a leading contributor on governance matters. We have a statement on corporate governance available on our website (*www.hermes.co.uk*) and there are a couple of principles I want to highlight from this to set the scene.

Our first general principle is that directors of public companies are responsible for running the companies in the long-term interest of the shareholders. Shareholders and their agents have responsibilities as owners to exercise stewardship of companies and, therefore, corporate governance should provide a framework where both parties can fulfil these responsibilities. Secondly, a very important principle is that a company run in the long-term interest of its shareholders will need to manage effectively its relationships with its employees, suppliers and customers, to behave ethically, and to have regard to the environment and society as a whole. Our approach to Social, Ethical and Environmental (SEE) matters is also included in this statement. And I am particularly delighted that the government's Company Law Review has adopted this enlightened-shareholder approach as the basis for the future of law in this country, as it distinguishes us quite significantly from some parts of Europe.

Now, let us talk about pension assets and equities. Life is full of unintended consequences. No one realised when pension funds were introduced in the past century that this would lead to a handful of countries dominating the world capital markets. And so, pension funds from seven or so countries own about a quarter of world equities. Countries such as Germany are now recognising the need to create pension funds, and what I think this means is that the proportion of equities that will be owned by pension funds is likely to keep going forward. But look at the changes in pension fund asset allocations to international equities, between 1989 and 2000. In The Netherlands, we now have 39 per cent, compared with 7 per cent a decade ago, invested in international equities. You can see the increase in Figure 7.1, where most countries show an increase, in internationalisation, except the UK which for many years has allocated a large proportion to international equities. So, what is happening is that pension funds assets are not only growing as a proportion of world equities, they are becoming more international. Pension funds are of course the ultimate long-term shareholders, investing on behalf of some members for sixty years or more. The long-term health of companies is of critical importance to pension funds and, as our figures show, pension funds are of growing importance to international companies.

That is the background. Pension funds also share a common agenda with insurance companies and insurance funds – mutual funds that invest the long-term savings of their clients. Collectively, these are the institutional investors that dominate share registers worldwide. All

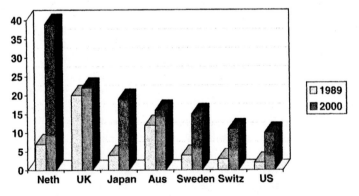

Figure 7.1 National pension fund allocations to international equities as per cent of total.

Source: Hermes.

institutional shareholders such as these are fiduciaries, which means that they manage assets on behalf of the underlying beneficiaries. There has been a gap in the stewardship of these assets, and it is this gap that we need to address.

The question is 'why is there now so much pressure for increased intervention by institutional investors?' Well, the first reason is certainly performance. Better-governed companies do outperform those with inactive shareholders. Secondly, executive salaries – they are out of step with the value created for shareholders, which has created enormous interest. There is then the wider stakeholder interest, and also governments Left and Right have accepted the model of capitalist wealth creation, but want corporations to behave without creating externalised costs (pollution, ethical issues and so on). Also, in the UK in 2001, we have the Myners Review (HM Treasury, 2001). The Government requisitioned this study, and the resulting report made it clear that it is the fiduciary duty of institutional investors to intervene if companies are underperforming, to bring about change and to either release value or prevent value being dissipated. Only in this way, Myners argues, can institutions do their duty and maximise their returns on behalf of the beneficiaries. And this duty applies whether the equity investment is a domestic or an international asset – there is no difference to the stewardship role.

So, let's look at this duty to intervene. It is global, but the methods of intervention must vary by country. Different jurisdictions have different ways of involving shareholders. And they often vary because of the legal system. Any discussion about what is appropriate for corporate governance in any country requires an understanding of the underlying legal system. In the UK and Australia legal rights are common in both countries – shareholders have considerable legal rights. They are not used much by shareholders, or at least they are certainly not used very well. In the USA, the rights are extremely limited; it is very difficult to replace a single director and impossible to create a vacancy on a board. What you have to do is put up an alternative director. In the USA you cannot call extraordinary general meetings, as you can with 10 per cent of shareholders in the United Kingdom, 10 per cent in France, 5 per cent in Germany. Apart from The Netherlands, effective ownership structures do exist in most European countries and several are much better than in the United States. The wise investor will also vary methods of intervention, because of different cultures and ways of doing business in different parts of the world, and this is something that Hermes takes very seriously. We now have over 30 people involved in our

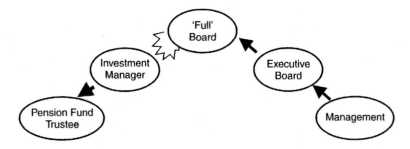

Figure 7.2   Chain of corporate activity.

corporate governance and shareholder intervention departments, which is more than any other institution anywhere in the world, and this currently includes 15 different nationalities.

So what does shareholder intervention mean? If we look at the chain of corporate accountability (in Figure 7.2), everybody understands that managers report to an executive board, which will report to a full board, which might be a supervisory board in Germany, or a unitary board here in the United Kingdom. But equally, the directors of the full board report to the fund managers, who are looking after the investment on behalf of the pension fund trustees. In any successful business, the board expects to be involved in the management and stewardship of the business, and similarly there is a way in which pension fund trustees need to be involved in the stewardship of the company; this is the issue that Myners has been addressing.

What happens if there is a weak link in the chain? The weakest link tends to be the one between the board and the fund manager, but there are also significant weaknesses in the link between the fund manager and the pension fund trustees; the contract between fund manager and shareowner often does not cover issues of shareholder engagement. So we have what Warren Buffet describes as the 'Gin Rummy' behaviour of fund managers – they throw away their worst card; fund managers who invest in underperforming companies just sell them. The UK Chancellor, Gordon Brown, has said that the financial system encourages investors to walk away from problem companies, and he has also said, 'we want to see shareholders sitting up and doing something.'

On what issues should shareholders intervene?

We are quite clear about this; there are four. It is very important to preserve the delegated structure by which shareholders delegate the running of a business to the directors. Shareholders should never try to micro-manage on day-to-day issues. This brings us to our first issue: shareholders should take a much greater interest in board structures and their composition. They should be asking whether the directors are up to the job that the shareholders have given them. Is there the right split of responsibilities on the board? The right number of independent outside directors? Is there the appropriate split between a chairman, a chief executive and a deputy chairman in terms of responsibilities? These are issues that corporate law always intended should be the responsibility of shareowners but this has fallen into disuse – how many shareholders just rubber stamp whatever is put in front of them? The second area in which shareholders should get involved is strategy. Major acquisitions, for instance, do require shareholder participation under current listing rules, but shareholders should look at business portfolio issues as well.

One of the techniques that Hermes uses on strategic issues is that if a company is underperforming, we will say to them 'we're only here because the company is underperforming. We think there is something wrong with your strategy. Please carry out a strategic review; use outside strategy consultants if you wish, use McKinsey or whoever, but please look at these ideas we have and come back to us in a few months with an appraisal of all the strategic options.' It's very simple, but there is not nearly enough of this sort of probing being done.

A third area for shareholders to be involved with is capital structure. Shareholder value is created when investment returns are greater than the cost of capital. Far too little thought is given to the cost of capital. Balance sheets are often too cosy, with borrowing too low or because directors have cash balances stashed away for a rainy day. We have engaged with many companies about returning appropriate amounts to shareholders to reduce the cost of capital and to allow investors to do what they are good at – allocate new capital to deserving companies.

The final area for shareholder involvement is in governance issues; this can range from whether the remuneration of the directors is properly aligned with the interests of shareholders, to stakeholder issues. For example, we engaged with Tompkins on the disposal of their gun subsidiary in the US (Smith & Wesson), with Premier Oil on their involvement in Burma and with TotalFinaElf, on their environmental record. These are all governance issues that are of great concern and can affect shareholder value. We might meet with management to discuss in detail our concerns and the changes we would like the company to introduce. Such meetings are often held in cooperation with other institutional investors. On the whole, there is an 80:20 split between routine voting and situations that require some direct communication with the company. Of the resolutions we voted against in 2000, the vast majority were on the re-election of non-executive directors who did not meet our definition of independence, in the context of the overall composition of the board.

Now, what is the current shareholder perspective in the UK? Shareholder intervention is not a new or passing fashion – it is about principles of good shareholder management; behaviour that was always intended to happen but which has fallen into disuse. The UK government's Myners review is a wake-up call for the fund management industry. It has admittedly a liberal approach. Ruth Kelly, MP, said in early October 2001, 'It is clear that the pensions industry needs to change the way it deals with investment issues. But the best way for this to happen is for the industry to take action voluntarily'.[1] Now, the UK Government is threatening to legislate to enforce the duty of pension fund shareholder trustees. In Hermes's view, this should not be necessary, because under common law the fiduciary duty of trustees already exists; it is just not being enforced.

Hermes has developed a commercial response to dealing with these fiduciary duties. Fund managers do not engage with companies to any great extent because no one has paid them to engage. Hermes has created Focus Funds, which invest only in underperforming companies. Traditional investors, the so-called active managers, seek to pick winners but owner investors seek to create value. But let us differentiate between the American-style corporate raider, and the relational style of the owner investor. The corporate raider undertakes his actions publicly, whereas the relational owner undertakes them privately. Secondly, the corporate raider acts for his shareholding alone, whereas Hermes and other relational investors act for all shareholders. Thirdly, the corporate raider doesn't have the market discipline institutions must have. The corporate raider will encourage short-term solutions, whereas the relational shareholder will have shares in the index for the long term, and just increase his holding for a while to have more influence in making changes. The corporate raider's objective is to manage the company, whereas the relational owner believes in preserving the delegated board structure. The primary objective of the relational shareholder is the creation of long-term shareholder value.

What is Hermes's style of engagement? Now, I have to say that there is a lot of Bob Monk's intellectual capital in the way that we have adapted the shareholder engagement product that he developed in his family business in the US in the early 1990s. What we now have, thanks to the combination of Bob's skills, coupled with the power, size and independence of Hermes, is a world-beating institutional model. This style of relational activism is not confrontational, it is about being firm where necessary, and overall having clear and honest investment object-ives. Management should see us in a long-term perspective as positive and beneficial – we invest in companies only because we see substantial upside, and because we have ideas to help create value. Our team has business experience and perspectives that open-minded boards do value. Recently, a FTSE100 chairman said at the end of a meeting with us, 'That is the best meeting with a shareholder that I have ever had in my career.' Hermes is an exception to other fund managers because our engagement team is a blend of fund management and corporate business skills.

The fruits of engagement

Much City opinion is sell-side research, and comment. There is value to management from properly expressed opinions of investors that invest for the long-term. I often say to directors, 'You can talk directly to us, you will get a much better, straighter answer, rather than going through what I call the fog of fees of City advisors.' Our only confrontations tend to be with individuals who have been holding back the will of the board. But if we do have to get confrontational, we have proved that we are prepared to do so. In December 1998, Hermes called an EGM of the poor performing Brazilian Smaller Companies Investment Trust; we removed an entire board and, despite the protests of the directors, over 90 per cent of shareholders voting supported the new independent board we proposed, and there was a 70 per cent turnout of shareholders.

What is the value of good governance? When I started five years ago, it was a gut feel that good governance added value; but there are studies now, some of them by respected academics, that do demonstrate that good governance adds value. McKinsey did a review that concluded that investors say they would pay 18 per cent more for the shares of a well-governed UK company than for the shares of a company with similar financial performance but poor governance practices (Coombes and Watson, 2000). I think perhaps more significant is the Millstein and MacAvoy paper in the *Columbia Law Review* in June 1998, the perform-ance gap between well governed and poorly governed firms exceeded 25 per cent of the return to investors.

But I am a businessman, and the proof of value to me is the perform-ance of the relational investment funds, the sort of funds that we call Focus Funds, since they started. Bob Monks invented this concept in 1992 in the USA, and the performance until he closed the fund was terrific.

It outperformed the S&P 500 in a period when that was increasing greatly. CalPERS, the very large Californian Pension Scheme, invested US$200 m with a firm called Relational Partners in the US. They are now our American partners. Their investment performance over five years has been truly amazing – an outperformance of over 20 per cent per annum.

The Hermes Focus Funds, the first of which was established in the UK in 1998, take a significant stake, in addition to the Hermes holding in the index, in laggard companies whose businesses are fundamentally strong, but where concerns about the company's direction mean that its shares are underperforming. The investment analysis takes a twin-tracked approach, based on assessing both the underlying investment value of the potential 'focus' company and the probability of effecting change through a programme of shareholder involvement. Once the investment is made, the Hermes Focus Asset Management (HFAM) team, which manages the Focus Funds, works closely with executive and non-executive directors and with other shareholders. HFAM uses its influence as an owner to help resolve issues that are hindering the company's performance, thereby aiming to create value to all long-term shareholders. The number of companies in any Focus Fund portfolio is usually limited to around 15. We now have an impressive three-year track record, our funds have grown to over £600 m. Our target is to

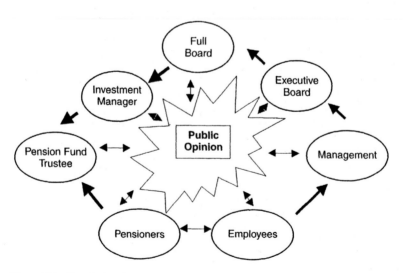

Figure 7.3   The chain of corporate activity revisited.

outperform by 5 per cent per annum on an average three-year basis; in our first three years the performance of our original investor, BT Pension Scheme's initial £50 m contribution, substantially exceeded this target.

Shareholder engagement works. It works where corporate skills are blended with traditional fund management skills in the engagement team. A good fund manager will pick stocks, add value in many, and lose in some. But if you add to the team people with various different corporate experiences and skills, you are creating an extra source of value. It is this extra source of value that differentiates the relational owner-manager from the traditional active fund manager.

Engagement cannot succeed without contacts worldwide; Hermes's contacts are of paramount importance.

But why are our contacts so good? Aren't fund managers just the stooges of capitalist money grabbers? Look at the chain in Figure 7.3 – we have now added the pension fund beneficiaries to the chain – they are the employees and former employees of the companies we are calling into account. Ours is an inclusive approach – a necessary part of ensuring that capitalism works for the people. And I think we ignore that at our peril.

Note

1   Quoted in S. Targett, 'Fund managers to come under tougher scrutiny', *Financial Times*, 3 October 2001.

References

Coombes, P. and Watson, M. (2000) 'New institutional investor survey puts price tag on corporate governance', *Directorship*, September, vol. 26, no. 8, pp. 1–3.

HM Treasury (2001) *Institutional Investment in the United Kingdom: A Review* (Myners Report, 2001), London: HM Treasury.

Millstein, I.M. and MacAvoy, P.W. (1998) 'The Active Board of Directors and Performance of the Large Publicly Traded Corporation', *Columbia Law Review*, vol. 98, no. 5, pp. 1283–1321.

Comments by Guy Jubb

I would like to discuss briefly Peter Butler's chapter. I note at the outset that the difference between being a collaborator and a fellow conspirator is often very subtle.

While Peter and I agree on many points, I would nevertheless like to address partly what he said and partly what he did not say. My comments are expressed on a personal basis and may not necessarily be those of Standard Life Investments.

In particular, I would like to comment about who is the weakest link in this chain of accountability. I think it was interesting that Peter, in the first instance, drew attention to the link between institutional investors and boards. Undoubtedly that is a weak link, but I suggest that, over time, it has become much stronger, particularly in the post-Cadbury environment. But one link that Peter did not dwell on at length was that arising when he introduced the pensioner into the scheme of things. Many of us are members of pension funds already. Pension fund trustees are accountable to a certain degree, but there is, I suggest – particularly in the context of ethical issues – very weak accountability between pension fund trustees and members of the pension funds themselves. One question which pension fund trustees need to address is whether, on a systematic basis, they need to engage members or sample their opinions as to quite what they are expecting of the trustees.

Conflicts of interest can be one of the big impediments to shareholder activism. Peter suggested that Hermes has no conflicts of interest. I would suggest to you that as we all have conflicts of interest, it is rather a question of how we manage them. There are other institutional fund managers – and Peter and I, I believe, share common minds on this – who are sometimes beholden to the hands that feed them, in terms of the corporate pension fund that generates their fees. Those fund managers have hitherto found great difficulty in managing their conflicts of interest effectively.

Turning to the issue of the asset distribution of pension funds, Peter discussed the significant investment of pension funds in equity securities. Looking to the longer term, I would just pinpoint that attitudes to pension fund investment are changing very quickly at the moment. Pension funds – as we have seen in the press about Boots Pension Fund – have recently moved from equities into fixed interest.[1] As pension funds find accounting regulations in the UK and elsewhere bite more significantly in companies' annual reports, the long-term prognosis for pension fund asset distribution could well be back into bonds rather than equities. Therefore, it may be that bondholders have to be the agents for activism as much as shareholders over the long-term.

Reputational risk and brand management are another aspect that has to come into the shareholder activism equation. As investment companies we have our respective brands to manage, and consequently we have to be very careful when we engage with companies and with the media. We need to be careful that we are not undermining the reputation of the companies that we invest in. Shareholder activists, particularly on ethical issues, have a very delicate path to go down in that area.

Last, there is the relationship between fund managers and NGOs and others who, from an ethical perspective, are seeking to find levers for change in terms of corporate behaviours. There are interesting questions as to whether fund managers such as Hermes and Standard Life Investments should engage just as much with Christian Aid, the World Development Movement and Greenpeace as we do with companies. And how should those NGOs use the power of modern communication to bring their messages home to us in a way that is both constructive and effective rather than destructive and ineffective?

Note

1   *See* John Stones, 'A new chemistry for pension funds', *Money Marketing*, 22 November 2001, p. 48.

8
Reading the Business Ethics Radar: Lessons from Shell

Mark Moody-Stuart

I was given the title of 'Reading the business ethics radar.' It's not exactly the title I would have chosen, but basically it is talking about the impact of events, how you respond to events and how you try to identify events before they become 'events'. In 1995 Shell was involved in major changes of our structure – we were changing what had been a manifestly successful organisational system which was essentially based on country and regional organisations, to a business-based organisation. And this is because the previous system was simply becoming ineffective and we recognised that. Almost everyone internally recognised it. There was unanimity on that; there was not unanimity on what we should do about it. Doing something about it was a hugely complex process and at the beginning of that great organisational change we were hit by two major events – one was Brent Spar and the other was Nigeria, and in particular the execution of Ken Saro-Wiwa.

Now, in both cases, Brent Spar and in Nigeria in general, we had considered that we had acted responsibly. We had complied with our principles – well-embedded principles that we had had for 25 years and that were accompanied by very clear guidelines. These addressed the requirements to deliver what we called 'an acceptable return' to shareholders but also – enlightened for 25 years ago – addressed all other stakeholders, or what we would now call stakeholders. And this was a great shock. In each case, we felt we had done all the consultation and that we had understood the government positions, and then all of a sudden you are in deep trouble.

In Nigeria, if we go back in history, for many years we had run a reasonably efficient organisation in what was a very difficult environment, a crumbling environment with almost every structure in the country breaking down. We did not bribe people, we paid people honestly, and we were fully aware that there were major issues with government, but we felt there were limited things that we could do about this. So this was a big shock to us, because there appeared to be a big disconnect between what we regarded as our responsibility as business, and what society thought.

And we – as we said in the first Shell Report – 'looked into the mirror, and we neither recognised nor liked what we saw.' (Shell, 1998, p. 2). So, being a systematic company, we thought, 'Well, we'd better go out and find what people actually do want.' So, we organised something to test and to find out what society all around the world thinks are the responsibilities of a major international organisation, and we did workshops in every continent, several in some, and these were done with 12 people (Shell people – not just from the top – from right down the company) with 12 outsiders – media, journalists, NGOs, government people and so on. And we asked them, 'What do you think about this, what do you think that major companies should be doing?' I went to one of these in The Netherlands, and I was thinking that we were going to be totally beaten up and that they would say: 'You have not done this' or 'You have not done that'. However, my experience was completely different. People were just fascinated, and they would say, 'We are delighted that you asked us, or appear at least hypothetically willing to listen,' and then they proceeded to talk about the issues and so on. Out of that, we went right back to our principles and said 'Should we make changes to our principles?' And we made three sets of changes.

One was in relation to politics. We had always had, for many years, a ban on any party political contribution, any political payments anywhere in the world, and we said in shorthand 'We are not involved in politics', and people outside the company said 'That is plainly an untrue statement – you are obviously involved in politics as a major economic actor'. We said, 'Well, that is not what we mean' and they said, 'Well, that is not what you said', so we changed it to say that we would retain the ban on political payments, but say that we would not be involved in party politics.

The second change was on human rights, and after huge discussion round the world with human rights organisations, we acknowledged responsibilities for human rights for our own employees and for the communities around us and expressed support in general for fundamental rights. These are now made explicit in the Shell Group Business Principles.[1] Principle 2 commits Shell companies to respect the human rights of their employees, to provide their employees with good and safe conditions of work, and good and competitive terms and conditions of service, to promote the development and best use of human talent and equal opportunity employment, to encourage the involvement of employees in the planning and direction of their work, and in the application of these principles within their company.

Principle 5 states:

Shell companies do not make payments to political parties, organisations or their representatives or take any part in party politics. However, when dealing with governments, Shell companies have the right and the responsibility to make their position known on any matter which affects them, their employees, their customers, or their shareholders. They also have a right to make their position known on matters affecting the community, where they have a contribution to make.

And Principle 2 goes on to affirm that Shell companies will act

as responsible members of society, to observe the laws of the country in which they operate, to express support for fundamental human rights in line with the legitimate role of business and to give proper regard to the health safety and environment consistent with their commitment to contribute to sustainable development.

We sweated over these principles, and we checked them, and made sure that our people in difficult countries could live with them, and in the end we published them.

Thirdly, we made a commitment to run our business in line with the principles of sustainable development. We did not do a great amount of testing on that and that is fundamentally the most difficult one.

The reaction of the outside world was, 'Yes, that is fine, and we think these are magnificent principles and you cannot do better, and the changes you have made are terrific, but how do we know that these aren't just words, how do you run your business in line with them?' And that lead to producing the first annual Shell Report published in April 1998, which is an attempt, in consultation with others, to report on how we perform in relation to our businesses and wherever possible to have this externally verified. Initially, we structured the report on the business principles, there were originally nine, and this became a little repetitive. So, after the first one, we changed to doing it in line with the economic, social and environmental triple-bottom-line mode, and merely referencing the principles as appropriate. That is the process we have been going through in iterations since.

I think I should say that, during 1999, I had personally a huge worry. Our financial performance at the end of 1998 and in 1998 was not good, and I was deeply concerned that we fix the financial performance because all three legs of the triple-bottom-line model are absolutely vital. Good performance in one does not allow you to underperform in another. Financial performance is important for a business. Indeed, it is just as important for an NGO to get their financial leg right, because if you do not get the financial leg right, you are out of business. If you muck up the environment, and you get the financial leg right you are probably also out of business, and in the long run if you get the first two right – you are impeccably performing environmentally and financially – but if you are not seen as being useful to society, I believe in the end you will also cease to exist. So I was very worried that if we failed on financial performance, many people in the world would turn around and say 'Look, this is because you took your eye off the ball, you started worrying about all these soft and woolly things.' That would do huge damage, not just to Shell but to the whole process – fortunately it didn't happen.

I want to highlight four things that we have learned:

- The benefits of consultation
- The power of telling things actually as they are
- The power of being able to say to everyone in the company 'this is what we do (or we do not do)'
- How you put this into a process, and do not try and fix it at the end, so that it is a process solution rather than, in environmental terms, an end of pipe solution.

But first let me just say something very quickly about our business because our relationship with our customers is very important. We supply energy products and chemicals, and convenience to our customers. And we know what customers want. They are very similar all around the world. They want instant, cheap, absolutely reliable energy available at the flick of a switch, the turn of a key, and they get very distressed if they don't get it. We also know that, at the same time, they worry about the consequences of that, the environmental consequences for both the global environment and the local environment. We also know that they want personal transportation – and that is a very deep human need right across the world – but at the same time, they worry about the consequences of that, the traffic jams and the pollution. They worry that in a few years it will take three hours to drive across Mumbai, and you will choke to death in the process – but that doesn't stop them wanting personal transportation. And thirdly, they want economic development, personal economic development and national economic development, and some of them worry about the differences within their own countries and between wealthier countries and less wealthy countries. They worry about how on earth are we going to bring these poorer people in the world not up to our standard, but to anything remotely like an acceptable standard, without blowing the whole thing apart.

Now, we also know that our customers buy from people they feel comfortable with, we know that from various sources. Buying convenience is one of their top priorities, price also, and so on, but their preference is definitely skewed to companies they feel comfortable with. That is, companies who share their sense of values, look like them, or feel like them when they talk to them. That is hugely important to them.

Going back to my four things that we have learned. Consultation is an essential part of the process; that whatever we do in our company, we go out and talk to those who are affected by it, whether you are putting in a major installation, or even just a service station. We used to just consult basically on what the customers wanted, and what the shareholders wanted. Now, we try to get everyone in the company to try and ask themselves 'Who is affected, and have I actually talked to them?' And it's not just a question of consultation – Come in, sit around, here is what we are going to do, and let me explain in great detail what it is and why it should not bother you. It is actually sitting down and listening and having a commitment, if they say something, that you will listen, and if possible you will do something about it. It is not simply information and engagement, you have to really open up and say, 'I am actually prepared to change what I am doing, to make modifications, maybe not even to do it', if that's what emerges from this discussion.

Secondly, telling it as it is, and preferably before someone else does. That is the essence of the reporting system that we have. We try to identify issues which are building up somewhere where we have heard about, very often which we have not solved, and we say 'This is the issue, here is the dilemma, here are the facts, what do you all think about it?'

This is the way that we think we can address it, not to say 'We have solved it, do not worry about it', but engage and give people the facts, and preferably then, in relation to it, agree to set targets, and report openly in the way we perform against those targets.

Thirdly, people really have to know that this is not just words, that this is something really important, and that you must really look people in the eye on a personal basis up and down the organisation and say, 'I really mean it.' And that our own people can say with confidence, 'This is what we in Shell do, or do not do'. This is absolutely fundamental if you are to build credibility with the outside world. You need to ask your own people: Do you have problems with this? You need to have discussions. What are the grey areas? For instance, if you go back 10 years, 15 years, anyone in Shell could say 'We do not bribe people', because they knew it to be true, they had examples, they knew what the systems were to prevent it, and they could say it with confidence.

When it came to human rights, some 10 years ago, we in management as individuals might have known what our position was, but we never talked about it, never discussed it, so there was no feeling for what the reaction would be. I hope that by now, people in general in Shell could say that we have an absolute priority for the human rights of our own people, we have a very strong responsibility to the people next door, to the communities, to the suppliers, and so on. We have, in general, responsibility for expressing fundamental support for human rights for the countries as a whole and for the world as a whole. On climate change, for example, it is very important that people within the organisation know what the position is on climate change, and can say, 'Yes, it is a serious issue; no, we do not have any solution to it. We do think that technology and Shell can play a part in the solution. We have set ourselves targets; we supply our customers with choices that will enable them to address climate change, we work on new technologies, we put the cost of carbon into our investment decisions. We are building training systems to make sure that our response can be most effective' and so on.

Lastly, process solutions: we need a management system in which we, like any other, can address these issues, and that includes an issues identification process. What are some of the issues that we have addressed as a result of screening? Well, I could take ship recycling, major big tankers, a very difficult issue, largely done on beaches in Bangladesh, Pakistan. This is an issue which we raise and discuss openly; What are the issues, what are we doing about it. What can we do before it becomes a major external issue? Child labour: initially you might think that in our industry reliant on heavy construction, it is fundamentally not a problem. We might say 'We don't know anything about it, no, we won't bother about child labour.' But then of course, if you think about it, there are suppliers' uniforms in service stations and the material we sell in service stations. Therefore it is an issue, and we begin to work on that. Indeed, child labour became an issue for us because alcohol goes into fuel in Brazil, bio-alcohol, which comes from sugar cane plantations, and sugar-cane plantations had a major child labour problem in Brazil. We then started to work on that notion. Animal testing: you can detect things on the radar, but sometimes you do not think that they are going to be a major issue. I think at the moment that with SHAC (Stop Hunting Life Sciences Against Cruelty to Animals) we are one of their major targets, not because it's actually a big issue for Shell, it is just that we are a very big and convenient target with stations all around the country. It is an issue that we had identified, but we have not necessarily brought it up to the corporate level because it was seen as a business issue, something for the chemicals business, something very small. I think that we have about two products under test with others in industry to meet legal requirements. We contribute to organisations looking at alternatives to testing and we actually have a very good record on it in inspections and so on. However, the issue took us somewhat by surprise.

What are the issues for the future? Clearly, for a company like ours, climate change is a big concern as is the globalisation debate, including local vs universal values. If you set about saying, 'We have fundamental business principles that everyone in the organisation and its joint ventures has to adhere to', you had better be certain that those values are acceptable universally, and that will require a lot of discussion. And how do you make sure that the local face of those values is completely in tune with that particular country? One example I can give is that of women employees in service stations in Sudan. Shell's Sudanese chairman fought a big battle to get women pump attendants in, and I said to him, 'Are you fighting this on behalf of our non-discrimination policies, or are you fighting it because as a Sudanese and a good Moslem, you actually think that it's the right thing?' And he said 'Absolutely the latter.' But it was fine, and government supported him.

Other contributors have covered some of the biotechnology issues, including the question of research on pharmaceuticals, drug patents, GMOs, which don't directly affect Shell. However, I do think it would really beneficial to have a good open debate on what the precautionary principle really means.

Lastly, you might think from this, 'Well, this is just a case of a big company listening to everyone: blowing with the wind, listening and saying "Yes, yes, we will do that", basically, you will fragment'. It is not. It is not management by focus group. You have to be prepared, after discussion, with people with a range of opinions, to say 'OK, we have listened to it all, we have probably modified our position but this is what we are going to do, and I am sorry, we are not going to do that or go as far as that.' However, the very strong point is that you hope that, by then, you will have a whole bunch of supporters out there including NGOs who will say 'No, that is right, that is our position as well'. You will actually have built support, and even those who do not agree with you will come to accept it. I believe out of this we can rebuild trust. One of my predecessors, John Jennings, coming out of what we learned from global workshops, said that the world was moving from a 'trust me' world, where big corporations were trusted, to a 'tell me' and then to a 'show me' world. And interestingly enough, when the Global Compact was launched, I heard a union leader saying this. I do not think he realised who he was quoting from.

I believe that companies like Shell can rebuild lost trust, but it is a completely different sort of trust. It has to be based on complete openness. What we heard from the GMO debate was, if you don't start with openness up front you are lost. You can rebuild trust through openness, by listening to people, and then achieve the dream (and we are certainly not there yet) that you become a company of choice. That is, a company people choose to work with or for, or that NGOs are happy to work with and collaborate with, that partners want to work with, and that governments want to work with.

Note

1   Shell's Business Principles can be found at *http://www2.shell.com/home/ Framework*

Reference

Shell (1998) *Shell Report 'Profits and principles – does there have to be a choice?',* London: Shell plc.

Comments by Bernard Taylor

The Crisis at Shell[1]

According to Charles Darwin, the species which survive are not necessarily the strongest or the fastest, but rather those which have the ability to adapt to changes in their environment. According to Collins and Porras (2000), companies which are 'built to last' also have the ability to adapt to a changing business environment.

The recent experience of Shell in dealing with complex socio-political situations illustrates Shell management's ability to learn from their experience. To quote the Shell chairman, Sir Mark Moody-Stuart, 'In earlier days we used to concentrate purely on the commercial role of firms. Of late there has been a great acceptance of the need to consider the environmental, social and even cultural impact of the companies. We now acknowledge that we have to take the broader aspects into account' (Moody-Stuart, 1997).

As Mark Moody-Stuart has explained above, Shell's learning experience was associated with the Brent Spar and Niger Delta where the company had apparently worked closely with the national governments concerned, operated scrupulously within the law and managed its business in an ethical way. However, having reviewed these events Shell's management concluded that in both cases their approach had been reactive and uncoordinated. Greenpeace and the other protest groups had outmanoeuvred Shell because they had better networks with Shell's customers, the media, politicians and with other activist groups. On the other hand, Shell had allied itself with the British and Nigerian governments and this had limited their space for manoeuvre.

The Camsea gas field

In 1996–98, Shell became involved in a project with the Peruvian Government and various local interests with a view to developing a world-class gas field in the upper Amazon region. Shell's management very carefully researched the environmental and social problems, and the possibilities of marketing the gas. This involved elaborate and lengthy consultation with various stakeholder groups. Shell defines a stakeholder as 'any individual or group which is affected by the project or can themselves affect the project'. Using this definition the company identified 350 stakeholder groups, 40 'primary stakeholders' directly linked to the project and over 300 'secondary stakeholders' who might have an indirect interest in the project. Shell carried out an Environmental Impact Assessment (EIA) and a Social Impact Assessment (SIA) and the company finally abandoned the project because, it said, of the difficulties of marketing the gas.

Clearly the project also carried a major 'reputation risk' and after the problems that the company had met with Brent Spar and the Niger Delta, the management was under no illusions about the downside risks attached to development programmes with complex environmental, social and political dimensions.

The implications for management[2]

Taking stock and taking action

Managers should learn from Shell's experiences in Brent Spar and the Niger Delta and they should take stock, re-evaluate their social responsibilities and decide how they will respond.

Issue management

The key points for action are summarised below:

Analysing the issues. The first step is to identify the public issues that are important for the company, its management and its stakeholders, then to determine which individuals or groups have a special interest in these issues and finally to decide what stage the issue has reached. For example, whether it is emerging and can be influenced, or mature and about to be dealt with by law.

Assessing the risks and the potential benefits. Management should then examine whether the company's reputation could be damaged and whether the company's operations are likely to be disrupted. Or alternatively, whether the company's reputation could be enhanced if it was associated with positive developments in the field.

Investment required. Having identified the important issues, the risks and the likely benefits, management should assess the costs of becoming involved in the issue as it develops and what the likely outcomes might be.

Staffing and advice. Campaigners for special interest groups and executives in governments and non-governmental organisations spend their lives in a 'political' arena. They know how to work through networks, lobbying and influencing others to achieve their ends. In general, business executives work in an 'operational' world setting objectives, developing strategies and plans, taking action and reporting back the results. For companies to be effective in the political environment, they need to acquire full-time or part-time specialists who think like politicians and who have the experience of dealing with complex political issues. All too often company chairmen, because they have been successful in business, wrongly believe that they have the experience and the skills to guide the companies through the political shoals. It is better to recruit people who already have the right networks and the appropriate experience.

Policies and programmes. The next stage is for management to develop appropriate objectives, strategies and programmes to deal with the key public issues in which the company becomes involved. This will require consultation inside the company, among some of the 'stakeholders' and opinion-formers. It may also be worthwhile to benchmark the company against other companies in the industry and in the region or countries where the company operates. In due course, the management and their advisors will probably produce policy statements and implement campaigns.

Assessments and reports. In some rare cases, it may be necessary for the management to carry out Environmental Impact Assessments (EIA) and Social Impact Assessments (SIA), or even to publish annual reports on the company's social and environmental performance.

Compliance. Compliance with the law is a separate area for staffing and advice. Public and social issues can be a minefield which requires the use of lawyers with specialised skills and experience. The whole process can become very costly and if there is any danger of litigation, management must be very circumspect.

Notes

1 For more on the background to this section, *see* Post *et al.* (2002).
2 For a fuller discussion of managerial responses to public issues, *see* Taylor *et al.* (1994).

References

Collins, J.C. and Porras, J.I. (2000) *Built to last: successful habits of visionary companies*, 3rd edn, London: Random House.

Moody-Stuart, M. (1997) *It's more than just business: Global Forum Conference, Konya, Turkey, 6 October 1997*, London: Shell International.

Post, J.E., Preston, L.E. and Sachs, S. (2002) *Redefining the Corporation: Stakeholder Management & Organisational Wealth*, Stanford: Stanford University Press.

Taylor, B., Hutchinson, C., Pollack, S. and Tapper, R. (1994) *Environmental Management Handbook*, London: Pitman Institute of Management.

9
Understanding How Issues in Business Ethics Develop: Lessons for Business

Ian W. Jones and Michael G. Pollitt

The scope of issues covered in this book has been considerable. Issues have been considered both from the point of view of how they developed and the nature of the issues themselves.

In the introduction, we raised a number of key questions about the development of issues in business ethics. The individual chapters have largely addressed each of these. However, we return to three of them here to attempt to draw lessons from across the chapters, namely:

(a) Who is involved in the development of ethical issues?
(b) What are the key stages in the development of an ethical issue?
(c) How may the development of the issue be influenced by business?

We address the first two questions by developing a model with categories of influencer and distinct stages in the influence process. We unpack the third question by examining the lessons of the model for effective business influence.

Influencers and the influence process

We summarise the main stages of the process of influence and the main influencers we examine in this book in Table 9.1.

The table indicates that there are three phases in the influence process and two kinds of influencers. The evidence from the individual chapters is that the influencing process can be described in terms of three distinct phases that are different in nature and purpose. The three phases have been identified as Awareness, Education and Implementation. The two kinds of business ethics influencers are type-A and type-B. Type-A acts

Table 9.1 Influences on the development of issues in business ethics

		Stages of the debate process		
		Awareness	Education	Implementation
Type-A *Influencers*	Events NGOs Media Popular feeling Politicians			
Type-B *Influencers*	Government executive International institutions Regulators Professions Investment analysts Investment institutions Corporates Non-financial Stakeholders			

principally in the public domain, namely events, NGOs, employees, media, popular feeling and politicians. The type-B influencers act principally in the private domain, namely government executives, regulators, professions, international institutions (such as the UN), investment analysts, investment institutions, corporate and non-financial stakeholders.

Awareness, Education and Implementation are elements of a process. They represent a simplified version of the phases of the process that we identify in Chapter 2 and a complementary representation of issue development to that revealed in the 'ethical issue life cycle' in Chapter 1. *Awareness* is where the matter becomes part of the public debate. Here, a swirling of forces that reflect the diversity of opinions intensifies. The heat of the debate rises to a point where something has to change, or be reconsidered. As a result, the debate can never be the same again. A maturing of the awareness stage sees stronger positions for and against become evident. This is clearly demonstrated by the GM crops debate, where the public became aware of the arguments between the NGOs and the bio-agricultural industry.

The *Education* element is where the issue is considered in a professional and detailed way. Education processes follow the classic scientific pattern: from the identification and definition of the problem; collection of data and analysis; development of alternative solutions; and choosing between them. The UK corporate-governance committees are the clearest examples in previous chapters of the education phase in operation.

The *Implementation* process is when the selected strategies are put into practice. The strategic decision emerging from the education phase has to be 'bought into' by those responsible for making it happen. For issues in the public arena, the strategy has to satisfy the strong opinions that crystallised as the awareness stage matured. Implementation is the culmination of the process, without which much of the effort could be wasted. Just as this is true of corporate strategy, it holds for public debates about business-ethics issues. On almost all of the issues we looked at, there was a point of buy-in prior to implementation. For example, on the child labour issue, companies in the sporting goods industry accepted the need to work with NGOs on implementing appropriate schemes to address the problem.

As well as being distinct, these three elements of the process are sequential. Awareness leads to education. The solutions developed in the education process become the subject of implementation. The distinct nature and logical sequence of the process does not preclude the possibility of overlaps between the elements of the process. New inputs in the debate, such as a public event or a telling statement, can occur while the educational process is taking place. Some aspects of implementation may start during the later stages of the educational process, as the experts seek to get buy-in or even to test the likely reactions. Debates about GM crops, child labour, the role of institutional investors and the public responsibilities of corporations are ongoing and responsive to events.

Two types of influencer

In Chapter 1, we suggested that we could identify a number of different influencers on the development of business ethics issues. In Chapter 2, we remarked on the fact that some groups had much less influence on the process than expected and others had more. On examining a number of different debates, we suggest that this can be taken further. Table 9.1 suggests that we can divide the influencers into two distinct types, A and B. This division is based on the observation of the nature of their contribution to the development of the issue. In their natural role, the type-A influencers are concerned with campaigns, raising public awareness, stimulating public opinion to form around a particular position. They are involved in the debate in the public arena. They are contributing to the swirl of public opinion. Politicians without government responsibility or acting on a party political agenda are part of this public-influencing debate. The type-B influencer is more expert, is more concerned with resolving the debate effectively and getting on with the business. Each has a classic role in contributing to a detailed solution, each has the ability to call on resources to investigate detailed solutions. Many of these influences prefer to operate in private.

The model suggests a spectrum across the influencers. The debates often start with an event. Disasters at the Chernobyl nuclear power plant and in the Union Carbide chemical production plant in India boosted the public environmental debate. NGOs and media bring the issues to the forefront. The public imagination is captured. Politicians stimulate the discussion and perhaps see political advantage from addressing the issue (as did Tony Blair in the corporate governance debate when he made a public statement during a tour in South-East Asia before the 1997 general election in the UK).

The spectrum continues as it crosses over from type-A to type-B. Executive government has a responsibility to investigate public issues and to act on political pressures, national governments in turn pressure international institutions for coordinated action, regulators are concerned with application in certain areas, and the professions are often called on to advise. Investment analysts, investment institutions, and fund trustees review these issues from their perspectives of financial stakeholders with a close legal relationship with corporates. Employees and other non-financial stakeholders with direct relationships with the corporates have an interest in the internal debate.

This ordered spectrum of influencers adds to the understanding of the roles and the interconnectedness between them. Clearly some of these influencers can act in different sequences of the spectrum. For the type-B influencers, professionals can work closely with corporates, investment institutions with executives in government. For the type-A, investigative media work can draw a subject into the political arena. However, the sequencing adds something about the natural roles and relationships between different influencers. An interesting example of the value of this sequencing is in indicating the relationship between events and NGOs. A campaigning NGO such as Greenpeace often relies on events to draw attention to its issues. Indeed, if Greenpeace did develop confusing evidence to attack the Brent Spar disposal, it could be said to have created an event to trigger public interest. The event/NGO link is potentially quite close.

There are occasions when those classified as type-B influencers behave as type-A influencers. Employees and other internal stakeholders protesting in the streets are acting as type-A influencers. Government officials entering the public debate may equally be switching to another type. However, the general model would appear to hold from the evidence presented in this book. The role and behaviour of a type-A influencer being public is fundamentally distinct from the role and behaviour of a type-B, which is private.

From influencer to influence

We can now combine the types of influencers and the phases of the process. The chapters suggest that the different types of influencers have differential impact on the different phases. We summarise our findings in Table 9.2.

The type-A influencers are highly active in the awareness stage. They are either public actors and highly skilled in influence or, in the case of events, public happenings. Such influencers are part of the public domain. They have skills in getting attention, generating feelings and making people aware of themes and big ideas. The type-B influencers would not appear to have much influence in the awareness stage. It is not their world, and most often they react to what that world throws at them.

On the other hand, the education phase gives type-B influencers the opportunity to contribute their expertise and professionalism, and make use of their superior financial resources. The type-A influencer can be rather out of his or her depth at this stage. Detailed comment is usually not their metier and is beyond them. For example, the media are not well suited to detailed comment but much better at getting attention. Detail and accuracy may be of secondary interest for them.

Table 9.2 Impact of influencer types during phases of influence

Influencer	Phase of Influence		
	Awareness	Education	Implementation
Type-A	Intense	Varied	Intense
Type-B	Reactive	Intense	Initiation and engagement

The implementation phase at the end of the education phase is the moment when the policy ideas come back into the public domain. The solution comes face to face with public opinion and public players. If feelings are high, then the solution has to engage those feelings. This engagement was best illustrated by the way that Sir Adrian Cadbury took the results of his committee to the public arena, making presentations to the CBI when its leadership had been hostile, and making his case doggedly in the public arena to counter press hostility or doubt. The type-B influencers have some role in initiating the debate and in taking the arguments into the public domain in the same way as Sir Adrian did. This may also be an issue for company public relations departments. Companies also have much to gain from engaging in the debate. In some instances, this can be to follow the example of the sporting goods industry and engage staff from NGOs to assist in the continuing implementation of corporate policy.

This table is descriptive in the way that it builds on what has been observed over the wide range of business ethics examples covered explicitly or implicitly within this book. There is also a normative element as exemplified by the successes and failures observed. The Greenbury committee stands out as a failure in the education phase. The committee, which was the key part of the education phase, appears to have failed to accept the intensity of the public feeling about executive pay and its desire to see change. As a result, it failed to address the problem in sufficient depth. The consequence can now be observed – the hostility to executive pay has continued unabated and the issue is coming back onto the UK political agenda.

This leads to the issue of the role and impact of particular influencers covered in this study. Events present triggers principally for public opinion. International meetings have become the focus of protest and debate. Brent Spar and Nigerian politics raised issues of corporate involvement in the environment and political parties. Economic recession brought corporate governance to the fore in the UK in the early 1990s. Ten years later we are seeing the emergence of a similar pattern of crisis and response in the US following the failures of Enron and WorldCom.

NGOs have been decisive in the business ethics debates. Christian Aid and Save the Children were seminal in bringing child labour to the attention of the public, engaging in the awareness phase, and this is what they are remembered for on this particular subject. They have been very active in monitoring implementation and clarifying the public debate. It is interesting to note that Christian Aid operates across the other elements of influence, the educational and continuing implementation.

In this regard, Genewatch (the UK gene research NGO) gives greatest emphasis to expertise and, in this way, probably has a greater influence on the educational phase than other NGOs. By observation and reputation and operating in the same environmental area, Greenpeace is a campaigning organisation operating in the awareness phase.

It has been noted that politicians acting in public often contribute to the awareness debate, as did the current UK Chancellor, Gordon Brown, in Opposition, on the executive pay debate and as did Margaret Beckett as a Government Minister in initiating the company law review debate. In this regard, the diminished influence of the political masters in the later phases of the corporate law review – the educational phase – is consistent with the model.

The role of regulators and government agencies has been exemplified by the US Federal Sentencing Guidelines for corporate conduct. This was a carefully considered US response to the concern about corporate conduct. The government agency involved used its expertise to shape the guidelines. This was a classic educational process. Subsequently, the US Department of Justice has fought a public battle to get the guidelines to influence company policy in what this chapter has described as the implementation process. Part of the role of regulators and government agencies appears to be threatening to use the law or defining and setting standards in order to effect meaningful implementation. International bodies such as the UN in the area of child labour and the OECD on the issue of corporate bribery have been very supportive of the educational and implementation phases. Such organisations have acted as conduits for the diffusion of considered best practice, and useful forums for putting pressure on lagging countries to comply with an emerging international consensus.

The role of the investor is probably a debate that is still in the awareness phase. Although, as indicated in the chapter, there is a considerable amount going on behind the scenes, the debate itself is probably still at the awareness phase. Parties are jockeying for position. New political or media initiatives could still be influential. A disastrous event could seriously shape the debate.

Corporates in the chapters of this book also show a similar involvement in the educational phases of the development of debates. The roles of Shell and Pentland provide corporate examples. Faced with being pilloried for lacking international integrity in the environmental and political arenas, Shell carried out its internal education phase and this is a special case of the model. However, the implementation phase was public and ongoing. The company committed itself to a new programme, it established processes which engaged NGOs and other type-A influencers. Pentland has followed a similar process of working through its strategy in consultation with NGOs and others, and participating in the ongoing debate.

The consequences of the model for business

Business ethics, as the term implies, is fundamentally about business. A key output of this work is intended to be how businesses can influence the development of issues which effect them directly. We now draw some lessons that follow from the above observations on the influence process for business itself. We take business to mean the commercial and corporate organisations that are the subject of debates in business ethics. While we have in mind stock market companies, the lessons can equally be applied to smaller companies and government-owned commercial organisations.

Business has limited impact in the awareness phase

A surprising conclusion is that in the awareness phase, with which most if not all of these issues start, business is relatively powerless. It has a hostile press. Even going back to the early Greeks, there was a hostility to profit taking, which was distinguished from exchange and transactions that were seen as necessary. Augustinian Britain was sceptical about the acceptability of business and trade, and absorbed business people only slowly into the political community.

In the contemporary world, many sections of the public have very high, and perhaps unrealistic, expectations of business. As sources of economic development, multinationals are expected to use their resources to the greater good of the community. As the bringers of technology, which may make other practices redundant, companies are held responsible for the destruction of employment. Those opposed to markets seek to attack business as an easy target.

Furthermore, business is pilloried in areas where there are other parts of society which have similar practices but are not targeted. There are several groups of professionals in society (accountants, lawyers, sports personalities and so on) who are paid substantial sums greater than those earned in the corporate boardroom, though perhaps to their credit with a greater correlation between performance and remuneration.

It follows that, at the present time, business may be on the defensive with respect to public opinion. If that is the case, then business cannot hope to win the awareness debate. Making public protestations probably appears to be special pleading. Indeed, business may be naïve in thinking that it can have any more influence than that proportionate with its size and, given the public regard, probably less.

Given that defensive position, it is critical that business responds to the awareness phase. It would appear that evidence in this volume suggests that the public relations approach of seeking to neutralise the damage immediately is the wisest in order to preserve some acceptability in the subsequent debate. For instance, Shell perhaps learned painfully the need to respond to public opinion, however misguided, by limiting the damage immediately, rather than entering the debate at the awareness stage. Probably of great importance is the impact on public opinion when a particular firm acts unacceptably. The damage that laggards do to business in general underpins the need for self-regulation.

Business has most to gain in the education phase

The research has shown the crucial nature of the education phase. In common with other type-B actors, the education phase is where they bring their expertise to the problem. In many ways, business is particularly well placed to have a significant impact on this phase because it involves problem solving, which is a fundamental business skill. Engagement in the education phase plays to business strengths. Business has access to the skills and resources needed.

The examples of Shell and Pentland have demonstrated how professional problem solving was effective in finding approaches to the problem that would be widely acceptable. In the policy domain, Cadbury achieved the same in corporate governance. Not engaging the debate in a problem solving way may have cost Monsanto dear in the GM foods debate. The ineffective engagement of the Greenbury Committee may have prejudiced the long-term outcome for business on executive pay.

Business can influence implementation

It is helpful to see implementation as bringing the results of the education phase back into the public domain. The solution has to confront public opinion. The implementation process is an occasion for business and other type-B actors to engage with NGOs and other type-A actors. Shell and Pentland provide examples of such behaviour.

Opportunities for business in cooperating with other Type-B actors

Other things being equal, like-minded people operating on similar tasks can cooperate better together. This would suggest that business could strengthen its business ethics case by working more closely with other specialists during the educational phase. This could mean working closely with government departments, international institutions or professionals. During the corporate governance debates in the UK, business may have failed to gain influence by not participating more fully with accountants and others in the committees.

There are opportunities for acting at the interfaces

The model suggests that there is an interface between the public domain, represented by type-A actors, and the private domain, represented by the type-B actors. In the model, it is interesting that the interface is between party politicians and the government executive. This is consistent with Western-style democracy. The opportunity for business as a type-B actor is that it may be easier to reach the public domain through the interface of policy making than by appealing to the public direct.

The different phases of influence provide more obvious interfaces. The interface between the awareness phase and the education phase places a high premium on the type-B actors being in close contact with developments in the public arena. This was referred to earlier as 'reading the radar'. Shell and Pentland, acting after issues had been brought to their attention, developed their own radar. This was based on having experts, including ex-employees of NGOs, within their policy-scanning team. This also involved education programmes through the company and adapting the vision and values and codifying the standards and the procedures for monitoring those standards in a way that corresponded to orthodox business ethics approaches. One of the values which Shell inculcated was that in Shell's world 'no man is an island', which could be taken in this context to mean 'manage the interface between the awareness and education phases'.

The interface between education and implementation is perhaps more difficult to generalise about. The size of the gap between public perception and the preferred solution produced by the education phase will probably determine the amount of type-B involvement in the implementation phase. Where there is a prospect of a gap, then interacting in the implementation phase is critical. Such gaps have clearly existed on the issue of GM crops in Europe and on the issue of executive pay in the UK. In both cases, the companies involved could clearly have engaged earlier to lessen the pressure on them at the implementation phase.

Table 9.3 The relationship between information flow and phases of debate, differential speeds of information flow

	National	International
Awareness	Instant	Instant
Corporate response	Some lag	Greater lag
Authorities response	Considerable lag	Very slow if ever

International application of the model

The research has had an international comparative dimension and has looked at issues that have crossed international boundaries. This international study raises the question of applying the model to international awareness, international corporate action and international regulation and, in particular, to the differential speeds in the global world (*see* Table 9.3).

In the electronic communication world, awareness spreads around the world instantly. Corporate examination and the operation of the education phase always takes some time. With the complexity of international organisations and taking account of cultural differences, the phase needs further time to take place. The gap between awareness and corporate response is, therefore, wider in the international domain. The greater concern is with the authorities. The authorities are usually slower in processing and implementing than the corporate sector. In the international domain, the problem is much greater, political differences and inter-regional negotiation imply that concerted action is difficult to agree on. The risk is that the rapid spread of awareness of issues compared with the slow response to the issue by business and the authorities will further undermine the reputation of business in the world and increase public frustration, as highlighted by recent anti-globalisation demonstrations.

Scope for further research

This set of case studies and discussion has provided the basis of a model which separates the phases of influence and the roles of influencers in the development of business ethics issues. There is a need for elements of this model to be tested by further work on the processes. The research agenda for business should involve identifying how it can have the greatest influence on the education phase. Of particular importance is the need for businesses to be quick to respond when the education phase is about to begin.

Conclusion

This book has reviewed several aspects of business ethics debates at different stages of development and has shown in detailed case studies what the ethical issues are and how they came to be perceived by the public, business and others. The case studies have given rise to a simple model of the influence process and the identification of influencers. This, in turn, has suggested ways in which business can seek to recognise the process and to do something to protect or even enhance its reputation. By concentrating on the education phase, business can maximise its influence by focusing on the phase of the process where its skill set has most to contribute to the debate.

Index

Printed in the United States
19112LVS00001B/74

9 780333 998106